The Living World of the Plants

The Living World of the Plants

A Book for Children and Students of Nature

by
Dr. Gerbert Grohmann

© Copyright 1999, 2013

Waldorf Publications
Research Institute for Waldorf Education
38 Main Street
Chatham, NY 12037

The Living World of Plants: A Book for Children and Students of Nature
by Dr. Gerbert Grohmann

Translated by Virginia Field Birdsall
Illustrations by Linda G. Lombardi after Dr. Grohmann's drawings

Editor: David S. Mitchell
Proofreading: Nancy Jane

ISBN: 978-1-888365-12-2

This translation was originally issued in manuscript form by the Waldorf Institute for Liberal Education, Adelphi University. Reprinted with their permission.
Please contact patrice@waldorf-research.org with feedback on this publication as well as requests for future work.

Table of Contents

Introduction	7
Foreword	9
The Sun and the Earth	9
The Flower and Insects Belong Together	10
How a Flower Is Formed	13
How Flowers Can Transform Themselves	17
How Trees Come into Being	21
The Willow	23
The Birch	25
The Linden	28
The Apple Tree	32
The Ranking in the Kingdom of the Plants	36
Mushrooms and Fungi	36
Lichens	41
Algae	44
Mosses	46
Ferns	50
Horsetails (Equisetums)	55
Club Mosses	58
The Needle-bearing Trees (Conifers)	58
The Yew	63
The Spruce	63
The Fir	63
The Pine	64
The Larch	64
The Juniper	64

The Families of the Flowering Plants	65
The Tulip and the Rose	66
The Violet	73
The Buttercup	75
The Stinging Nettle	79
The Dead Nettle	81
The Relatives of the Dead Nettle	83
The Bird Vetch	85
The Grasses	89
The Cabbage and its Relatives	93
The Dandelion	97
The Chicory	101
The Autumn Crocus	103
The Countenance of the Earth	106
Afterword for Adults	114

Introduction

It is a joy to see this book, *The Living World of the Plants*, in Mrs. Birdsall's fine translation, ready for the use of American children, parents, and teachers. It is a gift to all of them. Of course, there are many nature books for children. Most of them, however, couch a few fragments of information in fancy wrapping. They are written down to grade level. Grohmann has a greater aim. He knows what is wanted for children: a presentation of the plant kingdom in its genuine atmosphere—truth in the raiment of beauty. A description of the plant kingdom without its beauty would not be true. This is what Grohmann knows from his years of nature teaching at a Rudolf Steiner School. He succeeds in keeping to truth without sacrificing beauty, and he lets this beauty speak without sacrificing the least bit of accuracy.

These descriptions will hold good for later life. They are a large seedbed from which the maturing imagination of the student can always continue to draw its best forces. Even adults will feel this. Many have read this book as eagerly as any child and have regretted that they were not taught this way when young.

Besides conveying the true atmosphere of the plant kingdom, so closely akin to the child's world, this book has a farther-reaching aim. Working as it does on the whole being of the child, and appealing to his forces of feeling and will, as well as to his growing intelligence, this book helps to build up moral forces for later life. The young student who has breathed in the realm where nature's creative deeds appear in living shapes develops into a mature human individual with a creative imagination which extends into the field of moral action. The young student follows the changing forms which, playing around the lasting invisible archetypes, are yet never lost in lawlessness, and so he acquires a discipline which gives mobility as well as steadiness to his own moral being.

It is not yet sufficiently recognized how the difficult task of moral education is made easier by such nature study as is provided in this book. No moral "indoctrination" is necessary if, as happens here, a deeper layer in the soul of the child is touched, opening the springs of creative morality for later life.

Hermann Poppelbaum, Ph.D.

Foreword

A wise man, who still knew the secrets of the origin of the world, related: "From a giant arose Heaven and Earth—from his bones the rocks and stones; from his blood the rivers, seas, and brooks; from his flesh the crumbly soil; from his hair the grass; the clouds from his thoughts; the wind from his breath. But from the heart of the giant arose the Sun. Even today the giant body of the Earth is sustained by the Sun as by a warmth-giving and loving heart."

After listening to this tale, the children laughed and said: "That is a wonderful story. Tell us more!"

And the old man continued: "After man came upon the earth, the plants were transformed. God willed that men should see as in a mirror a picture of themselves—the perfect as well as the imperfect—in the plants, which serve them also for nourishment and healing. For this reason the plants have become so many and so different." Dear children: In this book, which has been written for you, you will learn much that is beautiful about plants.

Of course, all the plants in the world cannot be included in this little book. But if you have first learned a few of them well, you will know how to understand others better. But you must make an effort to penetrate into the secrets of plant structure.

So you should read with great care what is written in this book and read it often.

Then think over what you have read.

The Sun and the Earth

When the sun shines upon the earth, everything comes to life. The air, being warmed, begins to move, and in the water, too, all is astir. The sun-warmed earth steams, and its moist breath surges upward; the water rises, and the rain falls. Even the stones are taken hold of. Frost and heat burst them open; then, the water dissolves them and carries them along in its current. In this way the sun brings the elements—earth, air, and water—into activity.

But the sun can do still more when it works upon the earth. Its magic wand makes the plants spring forth in manifold colors, and each spring we experience anew the great miracle.

The plants are the children of the sun, growing upon the earth. The sun gives them their stems and leaves and forms finally the most beautiful part of all—the colorful, fragrant blossoms. Only the roots bury themselves in the dark ground, for they belong to the earth. But the blossoms lift themselves up into the light, whose creation they are.

The Flowers and Insects Belong Together

When you consider a flower, you see at once that it belongs to the sun. Creations so bright and sweet-smelling can come forth only from the light and warmth. In bad weather, when the sun does not shine, or at night, most of the flowers are closed; only those remain open which cannot close again after having once opened. But those which can open and close their *petals* follow the sun exactly—even the common Daisy. Thus, you see, there is something in the flowers that seeks the sun—something that longs to give itself up to the sun.

But when you think of the flowers and the sun, you should think, also, of those creatures which belong to them—the honeybees, bumblebees, and butterflies. Naturally you should not forget, either, the beetles or the flies.

These insects—so they are called as a group—act just as the flowers do; for they, too, love the sun. They fly about only when the sun shines, and if it is cold or rainy, they hide themselves. Only certain distinct kinds fly on warm nights. These night-revelers belong to those flowers which, also, at night breathe out a benumbing perfume. Butterflies and flowers have a strong resemblance to each other. The wings of the butterfly are as delicate and fragrant as flower petals. On the other hand, you could say that the flower petals seem like butterfly wings grown fast to the stem. The coloring of the butterfly wings comes from a dust as fine as flower pollen, so that you must be careful not to touch them for fear of rubbing off the delicate coating. The beetles, on the other hand, may be compared to the seeds of plants. They open their wings only in flight.

Butterflies and bees could not live at all without the flowers. They suck the sweet *nectar* from the blossoms and can never take nourishment directly from the earth. The flowers must prepare the food for them. But the insects take *pollen* also for their nourishment. The bees gather it and feed their young with it, but they change only the nectar of the blossoms into honey.

One can compare still further the flowers and butterflies. The butterflies carry on their heads long feelers, with which they can sense the flowers even at a distance. Though they cannot see them at all, they still can find them. You may think of the feelers of the butterflies as having become the *stamens* of the flowers.

Actually, one must say that flowers and butterflies are so closely united that they are parts of one and the same. Both are children of the sunlight and are brought forth from it. It is only when the butterfly lays its egg that it comes nearer to the earth. In like manner the flower drops its ripe seed upon the ground.

The seed sprouts, but what emerges does not in any sense resemble the blossom. The green plant must first grow, and with many plants this is a long process. The blossom comes last of all, only after the sun has worked a long while. So a new butterfly does not emerge at once from the butterfly egg. First, a little caterpillar creeps out. It is often green and must grow as a plant-like sprout. It also subsists upon leaves. Finally, it changes into a *pupa*, or chrysalis, which is like a bud. Out of this chrysalis, after a while, a gaily-colored butterfly is hatched, like a flower opening from a bud.

The stages of development of butterfly and plant may be placed side by side in the following way:

Plant	Insect
Flower	Butterfly
Bud	Chrysalis
Sprout	Caterpillar
Seed	Egg

Many flowers appear at a glance as butterflies bound to the earth. The colored butterflies, again, can be likened to liberated blossoms, flying freely about in the sunlight.

A Secret of Nature
Behold the plant!
It is the butterfly bound fast to the earth.
Behold the butterfly!
It is the plant set free by the universe.
—Rudolf Steiner

How a Flower Is Formed

The simplest flowers have the form of stars or cups. The number of petals composing them varies, but there are always at least three. Most flowers are formed on a plan of five's or sixes, so that a five or six-pointed star is traceable within them. But flowers formed on the number four also appear—though less often. The wild poppy, for instance, is one of these.

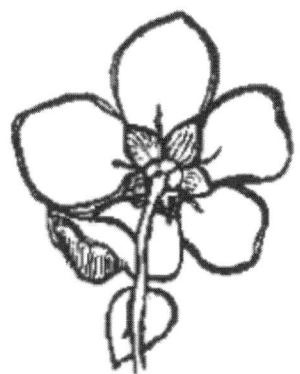

*Hypericum—
seen from the rear.*

If a flower has also a green calyx, the little leaves or points of the calyx always stand between the colored petals. It must, therefore, have exactly as many calyx-leaves (sepals) as flower-leaves (petals). There are, however, certain exceptions: for example, the strawberry has two calyxes.

The pistil stands right in the center of the flower, for it belongs to the stem, of which it is a continuation. In most flowers the pistil is divided into three parts—ovary, style, and stigma. The ovary is the hidden, lowest part. Later it becomes the fruit, and even in the blossoming time, when it is still undeveloped and small, it hides within itself the young seeds. It separates itself from petals and stamens—indeed, even from style and stigma—in that it is green like the stem. In many flowers several pistils stand side by side.

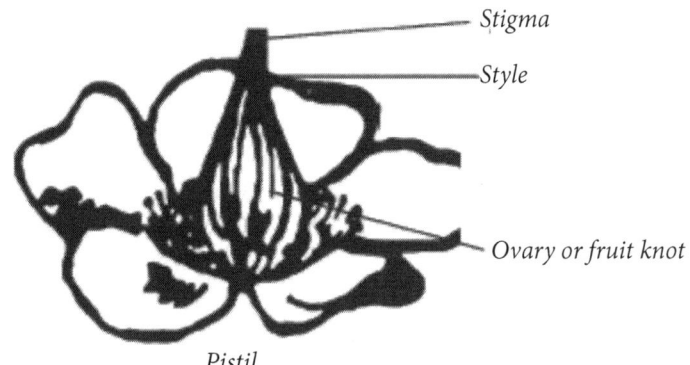

Pistil

From the upper end of the pistil springs the style, supporting the stigma, which may be split up into many parts. Several flowers, like the tulip, have sessile stigmas.

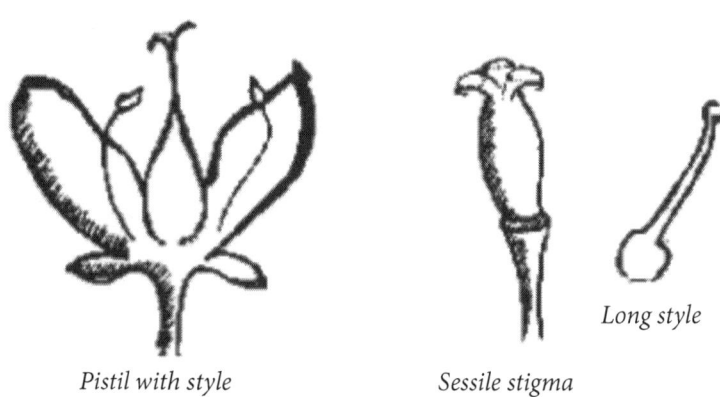

Pistil with style   Sessile stigma   Long style

If the pistils stand above the flower cup, they are said to be *superior*. Often they are under the flower base, sunk beneath it, so that only style and stigma are to be found on the blossom. Such pistils are said to be *inferior*. Apple blossoms have *inferior* pistils.

Hawthorne— superior pistil *Apple blossom— (lengthwise section) inferior pistil* *Apple blossom— seen from the back*

Around the pistil are arranged the stamens. There may be exactly as many as there are petals; often there are twice the number—or many, many more. The Poppy and the Rose have an enormous number of stamens.

The stamen is distinguished very clearly from the pistil, for it is not green, but very delicate and colored. The stamens have arisen from petals by a process of contracting and refining. In the Pond Lily, and also in many other flowers, the transition can be seen. Since the stamens belong to the *corolla*, they have a similar character. In many flowers they are yellow. They are generally joined to the petals and always drop when the petals drop, or wither together with them.

Stamens have their tiny stems, which are called filaments. These support the pollen sacs (*anthers*). When a flower opens, the anthers are usually still closed. Only after some time do they burst open and turn their pollen outward.

When the pollen reaches the stigma, the flower is *pollinated*. With most flowers the pollination is done by insects, which fulfill their important task without being aware of it, wishing only to suck the nectar or to gather pollen. There are, however, many plants whose pollen is carried by the wind. These are call "wind-pollinated flowers" (Anemophilous flowers). The Hazelnut, the Pine trees, and the Stinging Nettle are anemophilous plants. One recognizes them by their flowers, consisting almost entirely of stamens and pistils. Their pollen is dry; it could not otherwise be blown out.

With most plants pollination is of great importance, since, otherwise, no seeds could be formed with the pistils. In many plants the development of the fruit also depends upon pollination of the flowers.

In most cases the important thing is that the pollen is carried through the open air for a distance, however short, and most of the blossoms are, therefore, so arranged that the pollen of one flower can be carried only to the stigma of another of the same kind. The arrangements which bring this about are extraordinarily manifold and ingenious.

The plan is simplest with the anemophilous flowers—the Hazelnut, for instance, whose catkins (a cluster of small flowers on a drooping, tassel-like spike) generally consist only of staminate flowers. The pistillate flowers, with beautiful red stigmas, are in quite different places on the branch; so there is no other way but for the clouds of pollen to fly through the air, if the stigmas are to be pollinated. Many plants—as, for instance, the Stinging Nettle—are dioecious, which means that staminate and pistillate flowers are on different plants. There are, for this reason, two different Stinging Nettle plants.

How Flowers Can Transform Themselves

In many plants the petals are joined together, so that they cannot be pulled out singly; the corolla can be plucked only as a whole. Nevertheless, the actual number of petals can still be seen, for, although they are united, their tips have remained free. In the Bluebell there are always five tips, since every Bluebell has five petals.

It can also happen, however, that only the lower halves of the petals are united. In this case there arises first a tube or funnel, through which stamens and pistil stretch. The free part of the petals broadens out like a plate. Primroses and Cowslips have this type of flower.

When such a corolla tips over so that it hangs downward, then a bell results; but when placed horizontally, it can change itself in a very peculiar way. It is then no longer in the line directed towards the sun, but is placed parallel to the earth's surface like an animal. So it happens that many flowers become like little animals or at any rate develop a face—as, for example, the Pansy. But it need not always be a whole face; many blossoms have only lips or tongues, a throat or a mouth. The Snapdragon has a closed mouth; the Dead Nettle, on the contrary, an open mouth. In this case the palate is very plainly seen to curve upward like a vault, while the underlip hangs down. Many plants, especially fiery in their nature, have flower-mouths widely torn apart, out of which the stamens and pistil spring outward as if in anger.

The flower longs for the butterfly; the butterfly loves the flower—so each one seeks the other. And with the bee the case is similar.

Like Seeks Like
A fair Bell-flower
Sprang up from the ground,
And early its fragrance
It shed around;
A bee came thither
And sipped from its bell;
That they for each other
Were made, we see well.
—Goethe

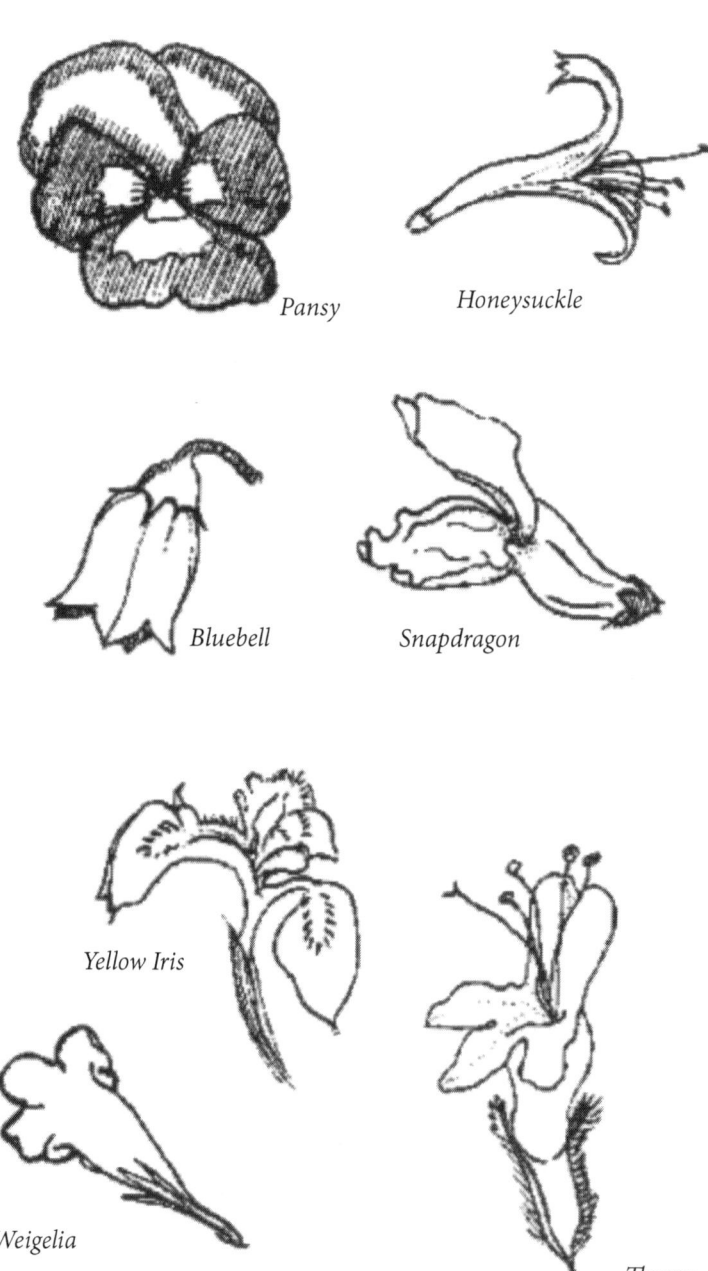

You can plainly see that the flowers and insects understand each other perfectly; you notice this from the likeness of their forms.

The simple corollas or discs lift their nectar and pollen toward the insects as if with outspread hands. The visitors then ascend easily into the dish and lap, lick, or nibble.

Matters are, however, not always so simply arranged for the insects! Often they must even struggle hard to reach the sweet nectar, for it is hidden in certain special places. There may either be tiny glands, cushions, simples, grooves, or bags—but the insects know how to find them!

In many flowers—as, for example, in Larkspur or Butter-and-eggs—the nectar is concealed far within a long spur, and the bees must force themselves deep within the blossom in order to get it. Who can ever describe all the wonderful devices of nature! Scientists who discover these for the first time have been filled with deep awe and the greatest enthusiasm, and so it is even today with each one who becomes acquainted with these mutual dependencies.

Many flowers have such long, thin tubes that only moths with their long tongues can reach inside—not insects with short mouth parts like bees, flies, or even bumblebees. The Meadow Pink is such a flower. Its flower parts close up to a narrow tube before they widen out to the beautiful, shining, red petals. The Meadow Pink is seen at a glance to be akin to the butterflies. It is a five-pointed star built of butterfly wings.

If you make careful observations, it seems to be true that flowers often admit only quite special insects and exclude others. The structure of a flower can never be understood without the insects which belong to it. One must always know how the bees, butterflies, bumblebees, beetles, or flies behave when they visit the flowers, and what movements they make. The forms of the flowers are quite different depending on whether the insects creep into them or only alight upon them.

The moths never go down into the blossom when they wish to feed but sink their long, extended tongues into the flowers, as they hover freely above them. In this way they touch the organs of pollination, which are pushed forward. Sometimes the mouth of such flowers is extended to form a long tube, which is split in front into lips. No human mouth can imitate such forms. The flower can do this, because it stretches itself out to meet the moth's tongue.

Such flowers and insects swing back and forth in their interplay. The careless person notices nothing of this, but to one who looks and listens many secret marvels reveal themselves.

How Trees Come into Being

The tree trunks are formed by the earth forces, and the branches —like plants which otherwise grow on the level earth—are lifted into the air and spread in all directions. A tree crown is, in reality, an assembly of numerous single plants, and when a tree bursts into leaf, it is as if plants sprouted overhead in the branches. When a Larch brings forth its foliage, it looks as if grass were sprouting on the boughs.

But the plants which form tree crowns are, to be sure, different from those below on the earth; the former grow out of soil which is already plant-like. If we should remove them to the earth's surface, then each one would have to acquire a root; but as nature made them, it is sufficient if all of them together have a root in common.

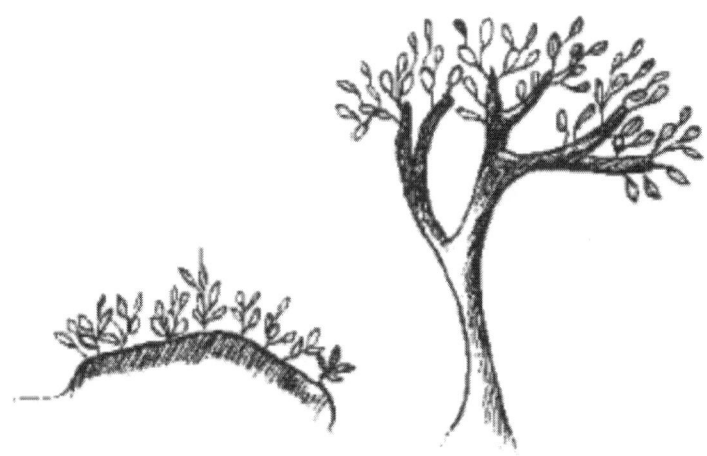

The sun can work much more easily with trees than with earth plants. For example, when a tree bursts into leaf, it need not form seed leaves, as do radishes, but it can just as well begin with large, fully formed leaves, and often the flower buds appear with the leaves.

All this can occur because the leaves and flowers do not arise in the earthly-mineral soil, but on the already plant-like, living tree trunks. It would otherwise be quite impossible for the foliage to come so quickly. In a short time a tree has its full leaf-dress and its blossoms, while a plant growing from a seed placed in the earth requires a much longer time for its development. First, the seed-leaves must appear; then the sun calls forth the small stem-leaves. Not until the root has grown sufficiently strong—reaching out into the earth—can the large leaves and blossoms follow.

The sun need not make so great an effort with a tree, for it is not necessary to begin from the starting point, since the tree trunk is already plant-like.

When one builds an ordinary mound of earth, it contains within it more living forces than occur on the level surface of the earth. Plants thrive more luxuriantly upon it; worms and insect larvae, which are contained within it, feel healthier. But still more life is present when the earth force rises still farther and builds tree trunks. Air and light can penetrate with much less hindrance and can work with much stronger effect than is possible in the usual earth-plants.

The way in which the earth works when it forms a tree trunk is recognizable as the same process that is present in the roots, for the root-force is identical with the force by means of which the earth calls the tree trunk into being. Root wood, too, is peculiarly hard—almost like stone.

You can easily see, especially in hollow tree trunks, how nearly related the wood of the tree is to the soil. When a trunk or an old rootstock rots, it crumbles into a mass, which looks like garden soil and has the same scent. It is called "tree soil."

Many insects and their larvae live in old tree trunks. They feed upon the rotted wood and go through their development in the passages which they bore, just as other insects develop in the soil. Beetles and their larvae, especially, are often found in dead tree trunks. Tree trunks may, therefore, be considered as outgrowths or outcroppings of the earth, or one might think of tree trunks as root forms jutting out over the earth.

The Willow

Willows flourish especially at the edges of brooks, ponds, and rivers, where the ground is moist, and the wind blows to and fro. They are not tall trees but mostly only bushes, for they are not able to form lofty and sturdy trunks. (This applies to the European Willows only.) In high mountains the Willows spread out their small-leafed branches thickly over the earth or flatten themselves on the rocks. It is, thus, clear that a Willow has but little strength within it.

Since they are watery, Willows grow quickly, but they easily break to pieces and split, and so become hollow and decay within. In the Willow you can see very clearly that a tree trunk is a kind of upturned soil. In old Willows the rotted parts can be scraped out with the hand. Only the wood lying just beneath the bark remains fresh and living, even after the inner trunk has decayed. Willow wood is very soft, and many insect larvae live within it—for example, the fat willow-borer.

Clipped Willow twigs can easily be stuck into the damp earth. Even if planted upside down, the roots push out, and after a few years new Willow shrubs arise from them. Basket-Willows are placed in especially wet ground, where they quickly put forth long shoots. Every two to four years these can be cut. Being soft and flexible, they are used for weaving baskets, for barrel hoops, and also for broom-binding. If Willows are pruned frequently, the top branches often become thicker, thus producing the pollarded Willows, which have no natural form of their own, but one developed by man. In a fog they make a ghostly impression, calling to mind the Elf-King and his followers.

The Willows have simple, undivided leaves. In the Sallow Willow (*Salix caprea*) they are broader, but in other varieties they are narrow and pointed.

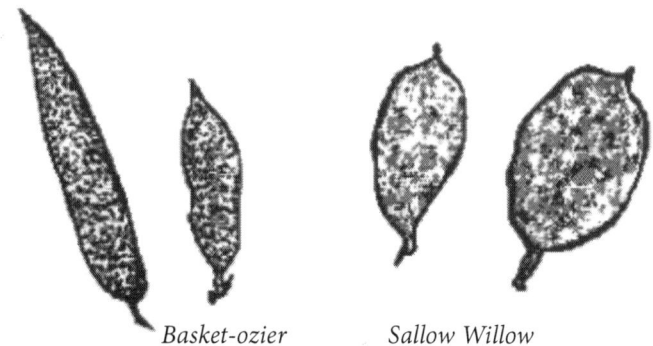
Basket-ozier   *Sallow Willow*

The Willow catkins are the flowers of the Willow. During the winter they remain hidden under a hard brown scale, but as soon as the sun's rays become warmer, they burst forth, showing their velvety covering of hair.

In a single catkin numerous flowers are closely packed together. These single flowers have neither calyx nor petals. The Willow is—one might say—too lazy to form proper flowers. If you examine a Willow catkin with a magnifying glass, you can clearly distinguish the parts.

The Willow is a dioecious plant. Never in a single Willow catkin will you find both pistillate and staminate flowers; there is either a pistil-catkin or a stamen-catkin, each kind being found on a separate plant. You can see the difference from afar, for the pistil-catkins are stretched out long and look green; while the pollen-catkins can be recognized at once by the bright yellow anthers on slender, extended filaments. A single flower has very few stamens, usually only two; but since there are a great many flowers, the whole catkin together looks like one single yellow flower. The appearance given in other plants by the petals is produced in the Willow catkins by the anthers.

The Willow catkins produce a great deal of nectar. The bees notice this, and on a beautiful day in spring they hum and buzz in the tree like a sounding organ. Those Willows which have only pistil-catkins are also visited by the bees, who need the nectar after the long winter rest, when all their stores are consumed.

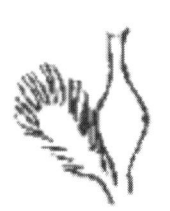 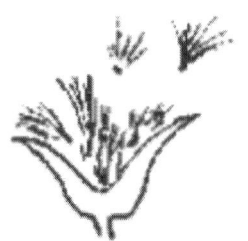 

Pistillate flower   *Seed capsule*   *Staminate flower*

Although the Willow is so quick growing, it cannot produce any juicy fruit. From the pistils come only dry seed-pods, which break open into two halves as soon as the tufted seeds are ripe. The wind has the task of broadcasting them. At the time of the ripening of the seed the Willow trees often look as if they were hung with cotton wool. This effect is, of course, due to the fuzzy seeds.

If a Willow wished to bring forth juicy fruit, it should not be so lazy. Wood and bark would have to become more pithy and also take up the sun force more strongly into themselves. But the Willow grows in the wind and remains cold and damp, yet it lets the fruit dry up. The man who resembles a Willow grows quickly and has a lively temperament, but he neither works fruitfully nor endures difficulties; on the contrary, he soon becomes decayed and hollow.

The Birch

The Birch (this description refers to the White Birch) is also a catkin-bearer, but is altogether different from the Willow. The Willow loves the water; the Birch loves the light and air. It gets along in the poorest soil and even penetrates far into the cold northlands.

The Birch gives an impression of youthful freshness. Especially in springtime, when it has just put forth its leaves, its light green shines brightly in the dark evergreen forest. You can very easily recognize the

Birch by its dazzling white bark, on which are coal-black scars. But its whole form likewise distinguishes it plainly from other trees. Its thin twigs are pliant and elastic. No other tree is so slender, nor sways so happily in the wind.

The leaves of the Birch are triangular and pointed in shape. You can see clearly that they are formed by the light, and it is this which makes them so graceful. In the Fall the Birches turn to a bright yellow, and a yellow dye can even be obtained from the leaves.

Leaves of the Birch

In comparing the Birch and the Oak, one discovers a significant fact. The Birch is really at its best when it is young; the Oak, on the other hand, reaches its full strength at a great age. The powerful trunk, with its wood hard as iron, the knotted branches, and the full crown are developed only in quite ancient Oaks. Young trees, on the contrary, show much less clearly the true characteristics of the Oak.

The Birch presents exactly the opposite picture. When it is old, it loses its fullness and its graceful growth; the wood, naturally soft, becomes brittle or rotten.

A Birch is most beautiful in the morning; an Oak, in the evening, when the sun goes down.

The Birch is not dioecious like the Willow. Pollen and pistil catkins are formed on the same twigs. The pollen-catkins hang loosely down, as in Hazelnuts and Poplars. They can be seen, even in the Winter, contracted in pairs on the branches. The fruit-catkins of the Birch stand erect at first and, besides, are much smaller. Only when the seeds ripen do they tilt downwards. The Birch is visited by no insects. In place of insects, it has the wind as companion. Therefore, the Birch catkins lack both perfume and nectar. As the pollen is wafted by the wind, so are the seeds, which look like little beetles, borne forth when the ripe catkins flutter apart. Each seed has two paper-thin wings.

Winged seeds of the Birch

In the Birch everything is light, airy, and full of movement. Since the Birch is so healthy, it has almost no insect enemies. But why, one may ask, does it form no real flowers? Why has it only colorless and scentless catkins? Is it too weak to produce fragrance and nectar? No, it is not too weak; it only acts differently from other plants. If, for example, one tastes young Birch leaves, one finds that they are aromatic. They have a covering like balsam. Who has not noticed the resinous fragrance radiating from the Birch? Even the bare twigs are fragrant.

The Birch, one might say, behaves in a very special way. Its leaves, buds, and twigs exude a substance similar to that which other pants produce in their flowers. In the white bark, also—peeling off in shreds—there is contained a kind of blossom substance.

This tree produces no nourishing fruit, but in the layers of its bark, rich in sap, it stores up sugar and oil. For this reason some native tribes eat the Birch bark or make it into bread when food is scarce.

In the month of May the Birch sends its powerful, sweet, and delicious stream of sap from the roots into the crown. If, at that season, one bores a hole in the bark, placing therein a little tube, the sap will drip out. Some tribesmen make wine from this Birch sap, or use it in its unfermented state as medicine, for it restores youthful strength to the sick. From the leaves, too, health-giving drinks are made.

We use the wood of the Birch as timber, or make brooms out of the twigs. For the people of northern Europe and Asia, the Birch tree is even more necessary for life. In these countries it is of such great benefit to mankind that without it life would be impossible. For the people of the North, the Birch is quite as important as is the Olive tree for those living in the Mediterranean regions.

The bark, too, has many-sided uses. It is skillfully peeled off and used like leather. Pouches, straps, drinking cups—yes, even shoes—are made of it. Larger pieces furnish roofing for houses, for Birch bark is impervious to water and almost indestructible, containing as it does a great deal of tannin. Naturally, therefore, it serves for the tanning of animal skins. When a beam which must last for a long time—a house-beam, for instance—is to be placed in the moist ground, it is first wrapped in a layer of Birch bark, so that it will not rot. In Finland the little children are laid in cradles made of Birch switches. These baskets are hung from the roof by long cords and made fast to a Birch trunk, so that the grandmother can easily rock the babies back and forth. In view of all these facts, it must be admitted that the Birch is an important gift to mankind. If at the same time you realize how unassuming and modest it is—that it endures frost and drought as can no other tree without suffering harm—you must indeed feel an affection for it. For it makes no show of its good qualities, nor does it boast of them. Yet it has much inner strength and beauty, for it is penetrated through and through with light. Anyone making use of it soon learns to treasure it justly.

The Linden

The Linden tree is a true companion and friend of man. Children often play under its branches, and many a person recalls with pleasure his childhood years passed in the shelter of an old Linden.

In the words of an old folk-song:

> By the well, before the doorway,
> There stands a Linden tree.
> How oft beneath its shadow
> Sweet dreams have come to me!
> Upon its bark, when musing,
> Fond words of love I made,
> And joy alike and sorrow
> Still drew me to its shade.
>
> (Translation from Schubert's Songs)

When the Linden reaches the height of its bloom, the bees are in a state of restless activity. A deep buzzing tone fills the tree, and the nectar flows profusely in the blossoms. Linden honey is considered especially delicious and health-giving. Not only the bees, but men also know how to treasure the Linden blossoms. You must climb up a ladder and take along a basket if you wish to gather them. Since they dry easily, they can be kept without difficulty. Many persons know how good Linden-blossom tea tastes and, also, that it purifies the blood and warms it through and through, bringing on a perspiration.

The Linden is the flowering tree in the true sense of the word. Its five-parted, tufted blossoms hang downwards in bunches. So the Linden reveals its earthward-turning tendency, and no harm is done, then, even though it rains, for the greenish-yellow leaves of the corolla still form a protecting roof for the nectar.

You can call the Linden a "honey" tree in contrast to the fruit trees. A Linden in blossom fairly oozes sweetness; its glorious perfume streams out in all directions. Even the plant lice which live in the Linden exude a sweet fluid. On many days the Linden leaves are completely covered with the "honey dew," as the sticky juice is called.

The Linden has nothing bitter, resinous, or poisonous in it. Buds and leaves are pleasant to the taste. If one chews them, they produce a mucus which tastes like bread. This mucus was formerly considered an efficient balsam for wounds.

The Linden is a tree beneath which one can well dream. Poets, especially, love the Linden, for it whispers good and beautiful thoughts to them. Our forefathers, too, knew how to treasure this trait of the Linden. In their eyes it was a holy tree, sacred to the goddess Frigga. Many place names still point to the fact that the Linden held a special significance in the popular regard. It was often planted where wise men and women performed holy offices or where wisdom was needed —as, for example, in the places where the judge made his decisions or where meetings were held. But on joyful occasions, too—at weddings and dances—people came together under the Linden tree.

Although the Linden is a quick-growing tree, yet it reaches a very great age. There are Lindens which are said to be a thousand years old. Very often we notice that the places where our forefathers once gathered were the sites of old Linden trees. One needs only to compare the Linden with the Willow to realize how venerable it is. The Linden leaf has the form of the human heart, and—as in the heart—the left and right sides are different.

Winter Linden *Summer Linden*

The Linden—not the Oak, as many think—is the tree of the German people. The Oak is, to be sure, strong and tough, but it is earthy and heavy. Connected with the force of gravity, its coarse fruits can only roll farther and farther downward. The Linden, too, has a strong earth connection, inasmuch as its fragrance seems to sink downward, but it remains at the same time light, without hardening. Its small fruits are furnished with a little leaf, so that they whirl about lightly and nimbly. Our forefathers considered the Linden leaf the sign of the free man, and the acorn the sign of the serf.

Fruit of the Linden

The wood of the Linden is white and soft. It lends itself especially to carving, and many splendid works of art are fashioned from it. Raffia is obtained from the bark by choosing branches as strong as a man's arm and letting the bark rot in water until the clear raffia fibers can be peeled off. Linden raffia is used to tie up garden plants, and from olden times twisted work of all kinds has been made out of Linden raffia—as, for example, ropes and bowstrings. And how safe must a warrior have felt when shield and saddle-work were woven of this material!

So this gentle tree has in it nothing that is harmful to mankind. It is friendly and filled with nothing but good qualities. The Linden is like a good mother—one who can tell fairy tales, too!

When the Linden leafs out, the blossoms do not burst forth with the leaves, as in the case of other flowering trees. First, the leaf-buds grow for a while, and only after some time do the blossoms come forth from the leaf axis. It is for this reason that the Linden blooms so late in the year.

In this peculiarity the Linden shows a deep-seated kinship to the Rose, with which it also shares its flowering time. The red Rose is the image of the pure human blood, while the Linden leaf imitates the shape of the heart. In the Rose, the flower is akin to man; in the Linden, the leaf.

THE APPLE TREE

The Apple tree is our most important fruit tree. Through the work of man it has become as we find it today in garden and in field; nature alone would leave it at the stage where it produces no edible fruit. The wild Apple—or Crab Apple tree, as it is called—has fruits that are small, with an extraordinarily acrid taste.

The Apple tree is also a flowering tree. When it is in full leaf, it shows its relationship to the Rose, but in a way quite different from the Linden. The Apple blossom is very similar to the wild Rose, although smaller. Each has five pink petals, and a five-pointed, green calyx, and there are many other similar markings. The five-pointed star, which the Rose blossom carries within itself, appears only in the fruit of the Apple—in the core. It can be seen when an apple is cut through crosswise.

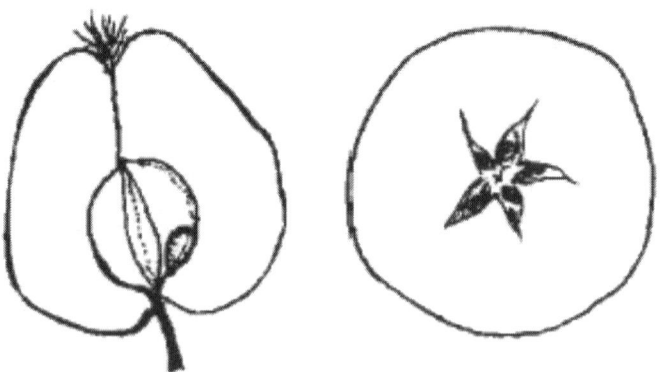

Cross section through apple. The core resembles a five-pointed star.

Rose and Apple tree are the parents of a plant family. The Rosebush, which produces an especially beautiful flower, is the mother; the Apple tree, which excels in the formation of fruit, is the father. The Strawberry is the child of this plant family.

But the Apple tree has other relatives, of whom only the fruit trees—the Pear, Cherry, Plum, Peach and Apricot, Quince and Medlar—need to be mentioned here. The Raspberry and Blackberry are closer to the Rose in their resemblance, for they grow like a rosebush and have tough thorns.

An important difference between the Rose and the Apple blossom lies in this—that the Rose, although so fragrant and delicately colored, produces no nectar. Strange as it may seem, the bees visit the Roses only to extract from them their very nourishing pollen. It is different with the Apple blossom. It gives nectar in abundance, showing that the Apple tree—in spite of other similarities—is richer in sap than the Rose. Otherwise, it could not produce its fruit. If the leaves of the Rose are compared with those of the Apple tree, still further contrasts appear. The Rose leaves are compound, while those of the Apple tree are simple. The Rose, which puts all of her strength into her beauty, gives special care to the forming of her green leaves. She is an artist in the true sense of the word, and man, who has succeeded in producing hundreds of varieties of the flower, has had easy work, for the Rose has willingly aided him in his purposes.

The Apple tree has also been cultivated for many centuries. But it would have been contradicting its nature to have changed it to a plant especially beautiful. The Apple tree sees its task in honest fruitfulness and wishes to be useful. Man has succeeded in bringing forth as many strains of Apples as of Roses. Both plants are unthinkable without man and belong to him as much as do the domestic animals. The Rose refreshes the soul—the Apple, the body.

It is clear at a glance that the Apple tree would like to make everything as simple as possible. Its leaves are, indeed, strong and healthy, but they have no very elaborate form. The trunk is short, the crown wider than it is high, giving the tree the appearance of being smaller than Lindens, Ashes, or Beeches. It must surely be intensely penetrated by the juices of the fruitful earth, since it bears these somewhat acrid fruits.

Even the bark of the Apple tree is of a fruity nature. This fact is known, for instance, to the jack rabbits, which sometimes become destructive to these trees in Winter. They come at night into the orchards and gnaw the juicy and very delicious bark of the young fruit trees. But you do not have to be a jack rabbit to find out that the branches of an Apple tree are fruity, for the sprouts upon which the flower buds stand are called "fruit wood."

The Apple tree has two life periods. The first is the blossoming time. This tree is able to bloom so early, because the flower buds have been prepared the year before. When the Apple tree flowers, it is more than ever like the Rose. To be sure, the Rose cannot bloom until later in the year, since it has no trunk, only woody branches. It must, therefore, first let its shoots grow and their beautiful leaves take form, whereas the Apple tree can begin at once with the flowers.

If the Apple tree had leaves to match its flowers, they would have to be Rose leaves. But the leaves of the Apple remain unformed and unfold only when the flowers have fallen, and so belong, not to the blossoms, but to the apples. This is the reason they are so simple. With the unfolding of the leaves, the second life period of the Apple tree begins.

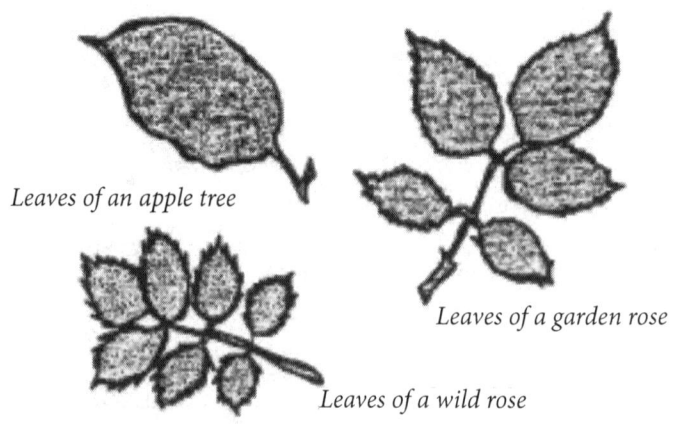

Leaves of an apple tree

Leaves of a garden rose

Leaves of a wild rose

The Apple blossom has an inferior pistil. It begins to swell as soon as the blossoming time is past, but even on the ripe apple you can see the tip of the calyx, as well as what remains of the stamens. This is called the "blossom" of the fruit. Since the pistil is buried in the flower stem, the apple must really be regarded as a fleshy and savory piece of the stalk.

Unceasingly, the earth sends her growing forces into the Apple tree. But hers alone are not sufficient, for the earth and the sun must work together in each Apple tree.

In spring it is enough if the sun only enchants the blossoms forth upon the branches. But if the apples are to swell and grow larger, the sun must penetrate further. It shines in the spring only from without, but in the summer it must warn the earth force itself, so that the earth can begin to drive the fruits outward.

Fruits are like drops suspended upon trees and bushes—drops formed by the sun-filled earth. Most drop-like in shape is the pear. But you can also regard the apple in this way. It is spherical, since it has swollen from the center out. In spots it looks as if it were about to burst.

So the Apple tree shows quite plainly the interplay of sun and earth. Naturally the sun, then, must ripen the fruits by shining sufficiently upon them and warming them through and through. They must become rosy-cheeked.

If you have once grasped the truth that the fruit of the Apple is formed by the earth, then you also know why the apple has always been regarded as a kind of picture of the earth itself.

The man who eats an apple consumes a little earth!

The Ranking in the Kingdom of the Plants

Not all plants are able to bring their development to completion. Many are to be considered as in preliminary stages of plant fulfillment, for they have not yet developed all their parts, or else cannot yet rightly separate them.

Such imperfect plants are called the Lower Plants, for they are often small and grow down near the ground, as, for example, the Mosses and the Ferns.

A very important step forward in plant structure occurs when, for instance, true flowers are developed for the first time. A plant which has root, stem, leaves, and flowers distinctly formed is called a Higher Plant.

It is especially important to understand why there occur not only Higher Plants, but also those which can be considered only as parts of the ordinary fully developed plant. The cause of these various stages of development is that the sun works together with the earth in different ways.

So we become acquainted with the ranks of the plant kingdom.

The Mushrooms and Fungi

It is no wonder that the sun does not trouble itself with the Mushrooms and Fungi, for they grow mostly in the shade of the woods and hardly come out of the ground as a plant should. Indeed, it would be impossible to set out a Mushroom in the garden as one would a green plant. It could not take root there at all. The green plants reach out with their roots to the rocks, for out of broken-down rock, earth-soil has arisen—meadow land and garden land, even loam and clay. The sun loves in a special way those plants which can grow in a mineral soil. It is able to give them the fullest leaves and the most beautiful stems and blossoms. Now you can easily see why Mushrooms and Fungi do not quite belong among the special favorites of the sun. They grow, as you know, in places where the sun penetrates only with difficulty; in fact, they have no need of the sun for their growth, and you can cultivate them—for example, the Agaric—in absolute darkness.

If you look carefully at the ground in which Mushrooms and Fungi grow, you will observe that they appear only in places where the remnants of dead plant parts are decaying. The Mushroom cannot flourish in a pure, mineral soil, but prefers one which is still half living. Mushrooms and Fungi have a much easier life than do green plants. Often, too, you find them growing on dead tree trunks. Only when a Mushroom is pulled out of its soft mother-soil does one notice that it is joined to a pale network of threads. These threads grow rampantly in the musty soil, like roots. They often branch out in a circular form from a center and from time to time send up Mushrooms. Large Mushroom circles of this kind are often found in the woods and are called "fairy rings."

Actually, the plants to which the Mushrooms belong have not yet risen above the ground. For this reason Mushrooms and Fungi have no leaves. In the case of the Apple tree the earth itself has formed an outgrowth—so to speak—and leaves, flowers, and fruit are high up in the light. But with the Mushrooms and Fungi neither the earth nor the sun has made any special effort. So, one might say, in the case of the Mushroom, the whole tree, with trunk and leaf-covered branches, is still mostly in the ground—still merged with the soil.

Only the fruits and blossoms of these plants jut out of the ground, such is the nature of Mushrooms and Fungi. A single warm night suffices for them to pop up in abundance. Need one wonder that many are poisonous, since they do not allow the sun to shine through them? Some Mushrooms—as, for example, the Puffball—are almost spherical or egg-shaped. You may liken them to fruit.

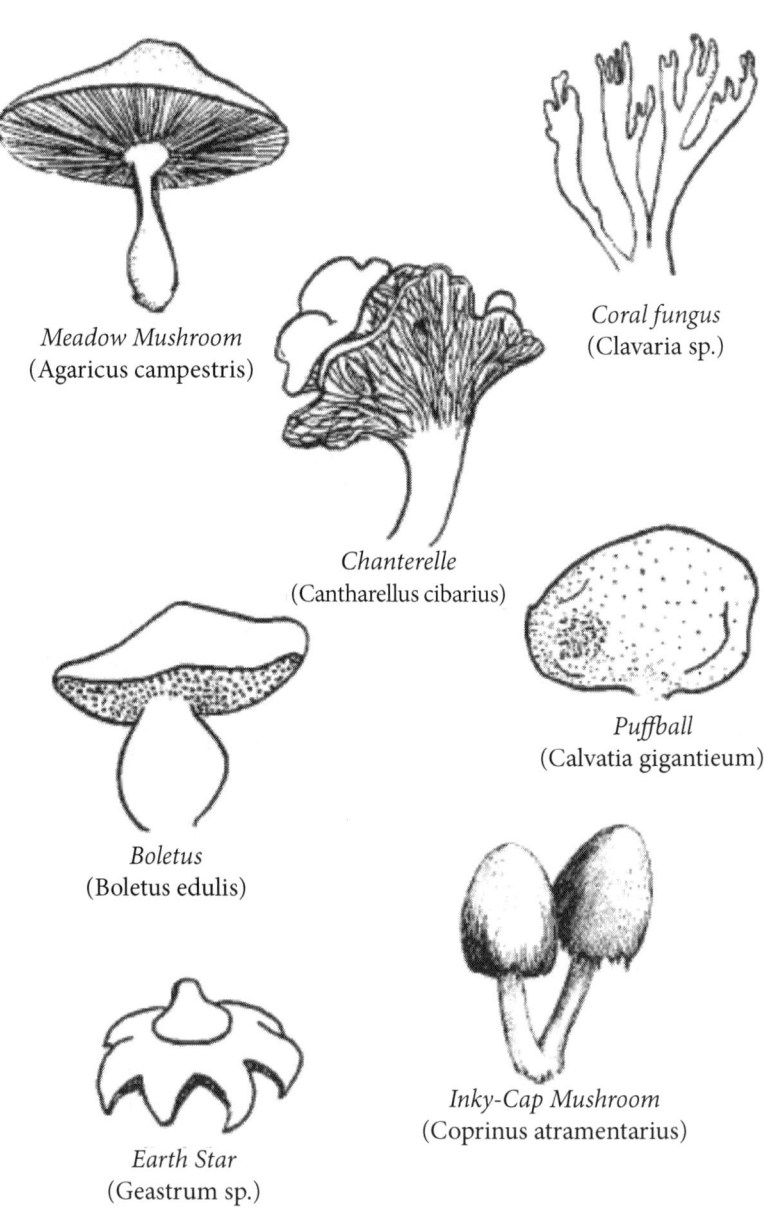

Various forms of mushrooms

Others have a stalk and a cap. All are fleshy, and the single fact that they are edible—if they are not sharp to the taste or poisonous—proves that they must be a kind of fruit.

Some Mushrooms, as, for example, the Chanterelle (*Cantharellus*), look almost like a calyx. The Mushrooms are, in fact, at the same time both flowers and fruit. They are too happy-go-lucky to behave as the higher plants, whose flowers come before the fruits. The mushroom has the fruit already within the flower, or, you might say, the fruit has taken on a flower form.

But the manifold coloring of Mushroom and Fungi does not originate from the sun. That is why they have such an uncanny look. They are the children not of the sun, but rather of the moon. Not a single one smells like a flower. Some, to be sure, have a pleasing, spicy aroma; but others, like the Stink Horn, infect the whole neighborhood with their odor of carrion.

Mushrooms and Fungi cannot properly make a distinction between pollen and seeds. If you place a mushroom cap on a piece of paper, you can see next day the design of the gill pattern upon it. If it was a Gill Mushroom, like the Fly Agaric or the Honey Mushroom (Yellow Armillaria), then you see the delicate gill-plates raying out from the center, for a very fine, dark-colored dust has fallen out of the lining. In the case of the tube-bearing Fungi (Yellow Boletus, Birch Agaric), the inner lining of the cap is perforated with countless seams; the lining of the hedgehog Mushrooms (Clavaria), on the other hand, is decorated with many little pegs. In some Fungi, for example, the Coral Fungi and the Goat's Beard, the fine dust forms simply on the surface. The interior of the Puffballs breaks down into a dark-colored powder. If you step on them, they burst asunder, and a cloud of spores rises into the air.

If the Mushroom spores fall to the moist ground, new Mushroom threads sprout forth, as if each spore were a tiny seed. It serves to propagate the plant, although it is as fine as flower pollen.

So you see that, in the case of Mushrooms and Fungi, not only are flowers and fruit identical, but pollen and seeds are likewise one and the same.

But you must not forget the most important fact! The flower of the Higher Plants open up towards the heaven and take the sunlight into themselves. They have actually been formed out of the sunlight. Mushrooms—creations of the darkness—open downwards towards the dark earth and keep themselves closed on top by means of the cap.

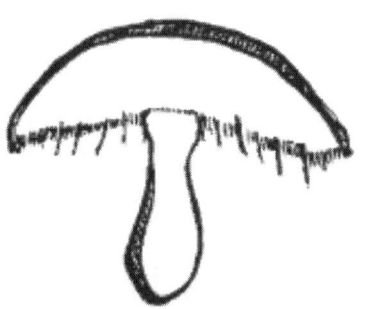

Mushroom opens downward towards the dark earth

Blossom opens up towards the heavens

Mushrooms and Fungi are the flowers and fruits of the sunless earth. What corresponds in them to the pollen is not borne by the sun-filled air but strives downward toward the moist, dark soil. No insect has any interest in mushrooms and Fungi. Flies and beetles, at best, come and seek the sticky slime. Since the flesh of the Mushroom is spongy, it is easily consumed by maggots.

Comparing Mushrooms and Fungi with other plants, one finds them somewhat like babies. They can do almost nothing. They can form neither green leaves nor stems—not even roots. They are quite unskillful and awkward. Babies cannot yet stand up; neither can the Mushrooms get a foothold on the solid earth, since they have no roots. So they are unable to stand erect by means of their stems.

Babies can, at best, only drink, sleep, and grow. Mushrooms can suck up nourishment from their mother-earth and likewise grow extraordinarily fast. They mix together everything possible—for example, flowers and fruit.

In babies the soul-light is not yet kindled, and so they, too, have learned almost nothing. Mushrooms and Fungi must grow without the outer sunlight, which gives other plants their stems and leaves. For this reason they, too, have learned almost nothing.

A little school girl once said: "It is because the Mushrooms are babies that so many of them, too, have milk inside them."

The Lichens

You often see on the barks of trees, especially on the weather side, and likewise on bare stones, a grayish, greenish crust in the form of scales; these are Lichens. You would not suspect that they were growing if you did not know it, for their growth is amazingly slow. In the damp mountain forests, threadlike branched Mosses hang down at times like long beards from the trees. In other regions, too, you will often see clumps of Lichens on the trees. These are not Beard Lichens, but Scale Lichens.

Lichens, like Mushrooms, to which they are related in many respects, grow out of a plant-like soil, such as the barks of trees, wood, pine needles, etc., but they appear also on naked stone and bare sand. This they can do, because they are dependent upon sunlight and so acquire a greenish color. You can find, in fact, that Lichens appear only in those places where the sun can penetrate easily.

Lichens form no roots. They hold fast, it is true, to the bark of trees or to stone, with fine, sucking threads, so that one can scarcely tear them away, but they take out of the air the substance which they need for food.

Lichens have one very remarkable trait. They readily dry up, or completely shrivel, without suffering any harm. Then, if it rains, or if only dew or mist falls, they suck up the moisture like sponges and are full of life again. How else would the rootless Lichens be able to subsist in tree crowns or on the sides of rocks, if they could not endure periods of drought without harm?

Since Lichens have no roots, they can have neither stalks nor flowers. Nor have they the power to stand erect, and when they grow longer, they simply hang down from the trees like loose threads or curly masses of leaves.

Lichens found in dry spots of wood soil sometimes look enchanting. Some have the shape of antlers. Others, such as the Cup Mosses, are like ruined castles. Reindeer Moss, which appears in great masses in northern lands and covers wide areas like a kind of cushion, has great importance, even for man, furnishing almost the sole nourishment of the reindeer. Still other Lichens thrive when the wood-soil is more profusely moistened. These are called Leaf Lichens, for they are larger and resemble grayish-brown rags fastened to stone or tree roots.

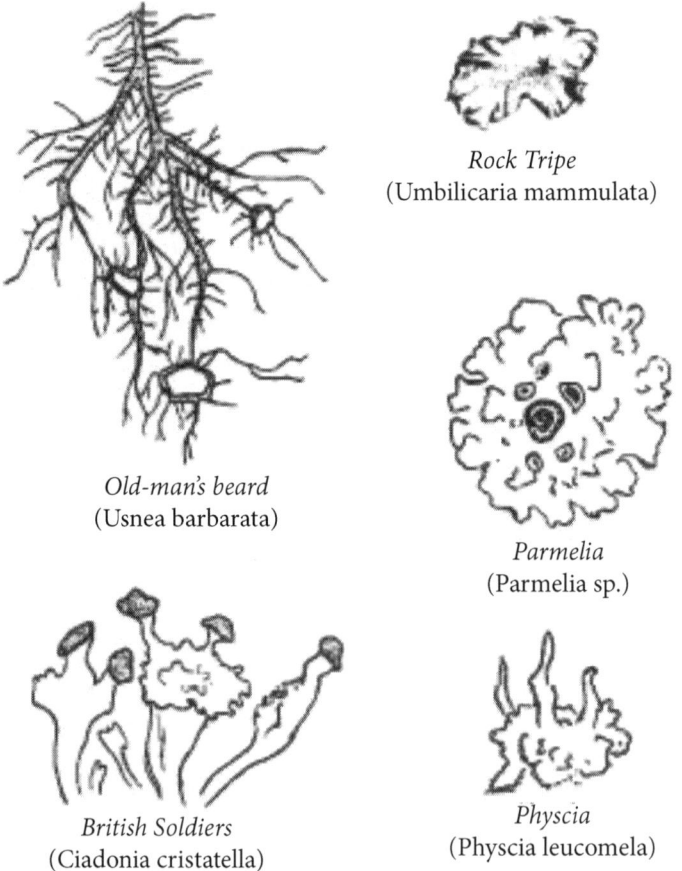

Rock Tripe
(Umbilicaria mammulata)

Old-man's beard
(Usnea barbarata)

Parmelia
(Parmelia sp.)

British Soldiers
(Ciadonia cristatella)

Physcia
(Physcia leucomela)

It is especially when Lichens are about to form their spores that they show how nearly related they are to Mushrooms. From time to time, indeed, a little Mushroom grows on the Lichen plant. Sometimes it is even so vividly colored, usually red or yellowish, that one wonders where the glorious, intense colors came from.

These little Mushrooms produce spores. Some are content simply to let grow from time to time a disc or little cup-shaped formation, upon whose surface the spores are produced. Lichens can also propagate their kind by means of little parts which separate themselves, are then blown or floated forth, growing up to new Lichens. So they spread out, gradually covering the forest soil or wood and the old tree trunks. Some Lichens look as if they could easily crumble to pieces. If you touch them, your fingers are covered with light green dust.

Wherever Lichens grow, the sun is at work; it would like to call forth plants, but it cannot penetrate deeply enough into the earth. The earth, too, would like to produce plant life. In the places where Lichens spring up, however, the earth has so little force that there arise those strange crusts or patches which lie only on the surface or appear like half-dried Mushrooms.

The nature of Lichens can be best recognized from the earth-zones where they occur. When you step over the timber line of the North, you suddenly come to regions where only Lichens and Mosses colonize the earth. The earth-force is no longer strong enough to form trees; the sun force has also become too weak, so that no weeds can sprout. Its rays fall slantingly upon the earth and penetrate only a little way into the ground. So the forms of plant life are limited to surface Lichens and extend no further.

High mountains also have their Lichen-zones. Where plant growth has come to an end and the naked stones are often made wet by the clouds, this strange form of life still flourishes and is almost to be regarded as a transition from the stones to the plants.

The Algae

Anyone who wishes to become acquainted with the Algae must go to the seashore. It is true that varieties of Algae appear also in the fresh waters of the inland, but, compared to those of the sea, they are small and insignificant. So one designates the Sea-Algae mostly by a special name and calls them Seaweeds.

All the plants belonging to the Algae are found in the water. They grow only when submerged and collapse if taken into the air. Algae are, indeed, true plants, for they have leaves; together they form a whole plant world of their own, which carries on its life under the water. Almost all plant forms found on the surface of the earth occur once more in the Algae stage, even if here they assume a perhaps vaguer form.

Standing on the seashore and peering into the depths of the clear water, one may fancy that he sees before him fabulous landscapes—meadows, bushes, and tiny forests—all swaying to a fro with the surge of the waves. Some kinds look like lettuce and are called Sea Lettuce. Others, again, remind one of Palms. Some take the form of thickly branched boughs. There are also moss-like Algae. Especially in warm seas, the wealth of color and form of the Algae increases enormously. Looking at the bottom of the sea from a boat, one marvels at their splendor. Many have no green coloring, but only red, resembling red corals. But some of them are brown or violet. You may imagine the abundance of color possibilities.

The Algae, in fact, are to be thought of as a kind of foliage. Whatever stalks or branches they appear to have are only drawn-out parts of the leaves. Their outlines, especially those of the broader leaf surfaces, are indefinite. You can easily imagine them being lashed to pieces in a raging storm. They are then sometimes torn loose in great masses from the sea bottom and float like islands on the surface. Sometimes little boats even get stuck in them.

Some Seaweeds imitate the higher plants. Many look as if they were divided into stems and leaves; others, as the Gulfweed, have fruit-like forms. Not a single Algae plant can produce flowers, because the Algae have no roots. Only their clinging discs, or very small sucking organs, hold them fast to stones or sand. And plants not truly rooted in the earth cannot produce flowers, for in this case the sun finds no point of contact with the plant. Jellyfish and other free-swimming sea creatures are, for the Seaweeds, what flowers and butterflies are to earth-rooted plants.

The Algae are formed from the sunlight. The interplay of sun and water gives them their particular flowing form. But you see how the development is carried further when the sun magically brings forth plants out of the solid earth, for it has already made the attempt to do this in the Algae. If you imagine the roots and flowers of the plants of the solid earth separated from the rest of the plant, and the leafy parts transferred to the water, you have the picture of the Algae world of the sea. The rigid stalks and tough leaves, to be sure, would in time become soft and pliant, for in the water everything becomes much more vague in outline. The sharp contours of the leaves would also dissolve.

The Algae of our inland waters are much more simply formed. They are green and are mostly thread-shaped, and so are called Thread Algae. Especially in the spring these slimy masses of threads appear in brooks, ponds, and pools. Later in the year they usually become dissolved. If you take them in your hand, they feel slimy, like wet hair.

The Algae include still other strange plant-like forms. Only their green color makes them seem at all like plants. They are to be found, too, in ditches, ponds, and pools, often even in puddles. With the naked eye you see only a green covering over the bottom of the water, and only by means of a very strong magnifying glass do you become aware that this mass is composed of thousands upon thousands of plant-like structures, mostly resembling minute dots. You might, at best, compare these tiny organisms to pollen, but never to a whole plant.

On damp rocks, gravestones, and the walls of houses, if they are kept moist, these microscopic Algae often settle.

The Mosses

The Mosses appeal to us, because they are so small. If you lie down in the woods and examine the Mosses about you, you discover for the first time their delicacy and the great variety of their forms. Never does a Moss plant stand alone; you always find a great many growing together to form a carpet.

Mosses are almost always damp. They suck up the rain water like a sponge and hold it fast. So they play a great role in the life of the woods. After the melting of the snow, or after rainy spells, the water does not run off at once, but trickles little by little through springs and brooks to the valleys. So the country is protected from floods, and the forest has on hand a continuous supply of water.

If one pulls up a single Moss plant from an old carpet of Mosses, it is astonishing to see how long it is. Some are almost a yard long, for they grow more and more at the tip and die off below. One is particularly surprised upon finding no rootlets. Some few kinds of Mosses have little threads which might perhaps be likened to roots, but most Moss carpets are so constructed that they simply continue into the ground.

Bog Moss plays an especially important role from this point of view. It grows only where there is always water. Mats of Bog Moss are very spongy. In both meadows and woods Bog Moss grows only in very wet places. It is easily recognized by its pale, yellow-green color. In the course of many years new layers of earth can arise with the help of Bog Moss. If you walk on it, the ground is soft and yielding; but if you are not careful, you may sink in and perish miserably—the fate of many a man who has failed to discover the danger of the moor. Bog Moss carpets are sometimes many hundreds of years old and of great size. In the course of time they have often grown over tree trunks and their rootstocks and have buried them underneath. If you dig ditches to drain off the standing water, you can cut the moss into bricks. These bricks, called peat, are used as wood or charcoal for fuel.

So, you see, Bog Moss is a plant which, although so small, forms a kind of soil.

Varieties of Mosses

Mosses belong very intimately to the earth. To be sure, they make an attempt to stand erect, but with only moderate success. Even little children must learn how to hold themselves upright. At first they can only reach a sitting posture. The Tree Mosses can stand up best. They look exactly like little evergreen trees, for they have tiny stalks with leaves on them, suggestive of pine needles. A whole mat is a little piece of woodland. Bog Moss can stand erect only because it is thickly packed together. It looks as if it had a flower at the top and reminds one of the Chrysanthemum or Edelweiss.

Other kinds of Moss lie on the ground as if they had fallen down. On examining them singly, one finds them like little branches, some like Spruce or Pine twigs, others with roundish little leaves and suggesting diminutive branches of leafy trees. So some of them are called Tree Mosses and others Branch Mosses.

Beside springs, especially in mountains and in very moist woodsy places, still other mosses appear. The Liverwort Mosses consist only of grass-green, patchy parts which simply lie on the ground and spread out by repeated fork-like branchings. Were they not grass-green, they might easily be confused with Lichens. They also have a marked resemblance to some of the Algae. They are called Liverwort because they were formerly used as a remedy for diseases of the liver. An acquaintance with the Mosses gives one a diminutive mirror picture of the plant world. All the parts of the higher plants are not united, however, in one specimen. Each part forms the basis of a special group of Mosses of its own pattern, so that the varieties of mosses might be divided as follows:

      Stems—Tree Mosses
      Branches—Twig Mosses
      Leaves—Liverworts
      Flowers—Bog Mosses

Contemplating the world of the Mosses in a moist mountain valley, you find yourself being led in thought finally to a kind of tropical primeval forest, for the Mosses do in miniature what the higher plants can do only in a primeval forest, where the force of growth has reached its highest point. Not only is the ground bedecked with plants, but on tree trunks and roots, too, there is everywhere an exuberant growth. Yes, even in the branches Moss plants hang like Orchids in a tropical forest.

What a wonder world exists in this realm! A famous Moss investigator once set himself the task of collecting and pressing the various mosses, which he then assembled into landscape pictures, showing that all the plant forms of the earth are present again in miniature in the world of the Mosses. On one sheet were assembled those Mosses that look like virgin forest growths; on another, varieties of Palms together built an oasis, etc. Anyone so wishing can make a similar collection.

Although they are very small, Mosses can accomplish more than Algae. It is plain that they would like to stand upright. Although they have no true flowers, still they are able to form that part of the flower that belongs to the stem, that is, the seedpod. The anthers also look mostly like parts of the stem. Anyone who has often examined mosses knows the strange little pods which grow on them. They are long-stemmed —the stem is called the seta—and the little pod is at first covered with a fringed, pointed cap. In the Tree Mosses the stemmed seedpod springs from the summit of the sprout; in the Branch Mosses, it springs simply from the side.

Hairy-cap moss with spore capsule.

Of course, this pod is the spore-sac of the Moss. You might say, too, that in the Mosses the seed is merged with the pollen grain, as in the case of all plants that produce spores. Yet it is truly a kind of seedpod. It may be thought of as a kind of pollen-vessel, although it actually contains not pollen but spores.

The caps can be pulled off, but later they fall off themselves to the ground. The spore capsule has a lid which must spring open when the spores are ready to be scattered. This can happen only in dry weather. The spore sacs of the Bog Moss are small and seldom visible. In the Liverworts the strangest structures appear in place of the spore sacs. These can best be compared to little green umbrellas. They scatter spores, as do the Cap Mushrooms, from the underside.

Whoever carefully examines a number of Mosses will discover many a surprising miracle. Though the Mosses are so small, they are very beautifully formed and with the greatest care.

The Ferns

There are three groups of Fern plants, each of which has a very different appearance and must be considered separately.

The most important are the Ferns proper. Everyone knows them, for they have such beautiful leaves.

The Horsetails (Equisetums), also well-known, are distinguished by the fact that they have no leaves at all, but are composed of mere stalk-like units.

The last group, the Club Mosses (Lycopodiums), are less known, since they are seldom found. They are chiefly interesting, because they played a very important role in primeval times.

The Ferns are in themselves a replica of the whole plant world. They are the descendants of much larger, similar plants, which were formerly much more numerous and elaborate. Indeed, there was a time when Fern plants were almost alone on the earth. It was that period in the earth's development when coal also came into being, called, therefore, the Carboniferous Period. The petrified remains of primeval Fern plants are still found in great masses in the seams of coal-pits.

Today ferns constitute only a small portion of the vegetation of the earth. At their best they still form great Fern forests in warm countries. However, if they disappeared entirely from the plant world of today, the landscape would scarcely be changed.

Ferns are flowerless plants. How peculiar the earth must have looked, teeming with that vegetation of giant Horsetails and mighty tree trunks! Not a flower was to be found, and, of course, while this state of things lasted, no butterflies flew about either. Only dragonflies and grasshoppers, which, indeed, bear kinship to the Horsetails, lived among the plants of that ancient time. It was misty and rainy, and the ground was miry and water-soaked. From time to time floods came and inundated the land, covering everything with mud and clay. At that time man had not yet set foot upon the earth, nor had the animals of today yet come into being. They would not have been able to live at all under such conditions.

Most of the Ferns grow in the woods. They love the moist wood-soil and the shade. In winter they die down, and you find, where a Fern plant has stood, only the remnants of leaves. Under the earth, however, the rootstock sleeps.

As soon as the fronds, or Fern leaves, burst forth from the rootstock which has carried them over the winter, you can at once easily distinguish a Fern from any other plant. Only round knobs, sheathed in brown scales, appear at first above the earth. But, on examining them more closely, you notice that they are rolled up like snails. The most delicate parts are quite within, and growth proceeds from the center of the snail, so that the fronds are gradually unrolled. Ferns, therefore, only appear to sprout out of the earth; actually they spring from the leaf spirals.

The Fern fronds are mostly divided like feathers. The leaflets may be again divided, and so on. If the fronds are compound, first the midrib (rachis) unrolls. On the left and right sides of this rachis sit real little spirals, which later unfurl into the side-leaflets (pinnae). The larger the whole frond is, the more clearly you can discern the beautiful picture. You can see the process at its best in the Tree Ferns of foreign lands, which are often cultivated in hothouses. The Tree Ferns look almost like palms, for they are raised up into the air on trunks. Naturally a Tree Fern is at once recognizable by its leaf spirals. Its fronds are often formed in an indescribably ingenious way, so that you never cease to wonder at them.

Since the sun bestows no blossoms upon the Ferns, it takes greater pains with their fronds, repeatedly dividing them and placing them upon long stems. In all nature the Ferns are the first growing things resembling true plants. They grow up into the open air and have a rootstock in the ground. So the plants of the Fern level are the first which could say of themselves: "We are real plants." This is just like when a child says "I" for the first time, referring to himself.

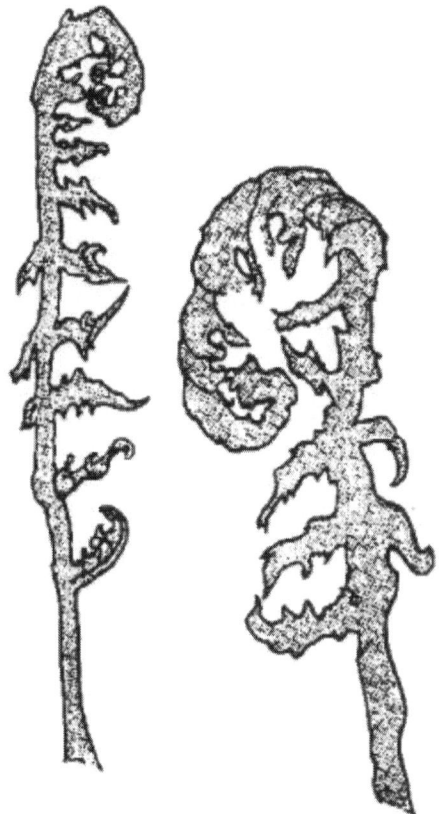

Two fern fronds unfurling

It is quite obvious that the Ferns would very much like to be flowering plants; for they imitate in their green fronds much that the higher plants bring to fullness in their blossoms. But since the Ferns are only leaf-plants and have no stalks, they can imitate only those parts of the flower which belong to the leaves, namely, corolla and stamens, but not stem and pistil. So, for example, you often see Ferns with their fronds so placed that together they form a great funnel. You might then imagine that you had before you a huge corolla. In this way some Ferns imitate flowers.

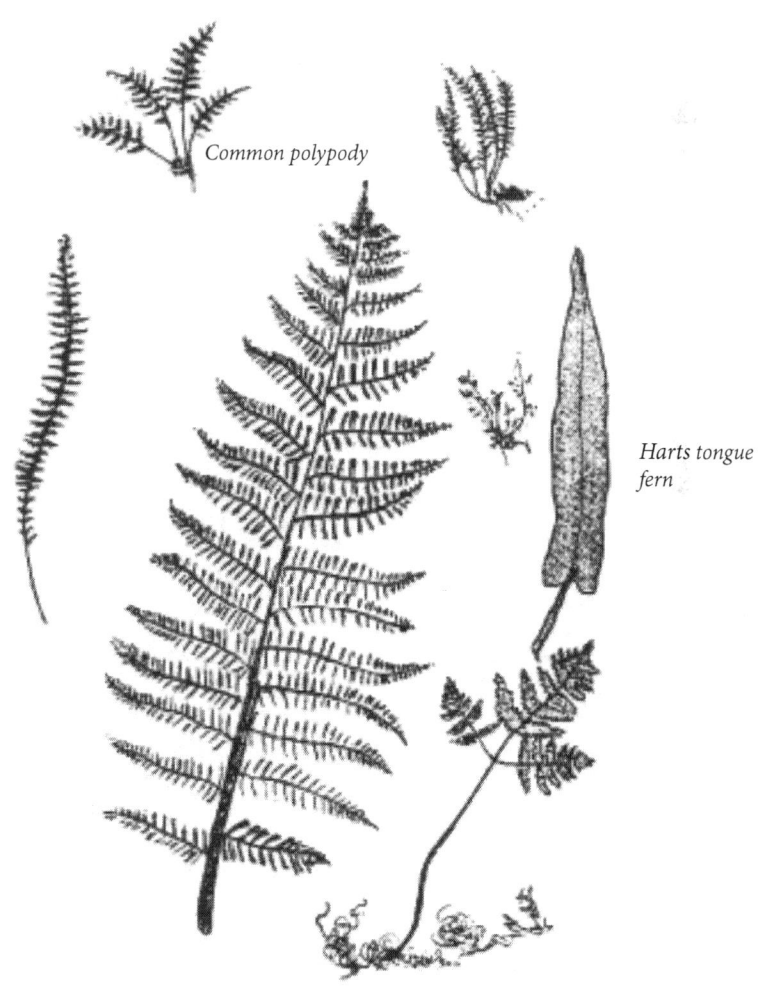

Common polypody

Harts tongue fern

Still more remarkable discoveries may be made if one picks a Fern in the summertime and examines its underside. Here it is studded with all sorts of brown patterns—little dots, stripes, etc. A wonderful order is here revealed, and each kind of Fern has a pattern in some way different from all others. Some fronds appear as if crusted on the underside. In the Brakes only the frond edges are colored brown and rolled in.

If you place such a frond on a piece of white paper and leave it undisturbed for some hours, then when you carefully lift it off again, you find the design traced on the paper. A very fine brown dust has fallen out—the spores of the Fern.

So, you see, the Ferns are still related through their spores to the Mushrooms, Lichens, and Mosses. They form their spores simply on the underside of the frond, as if blown there by the wind.

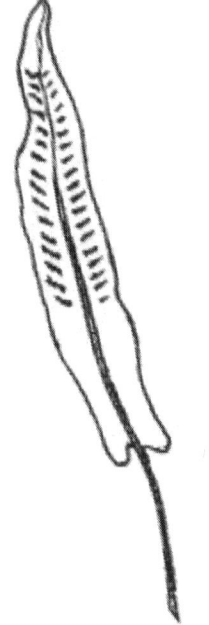

Harts tongue fern with striped pattern of spore capsules.

If the spores fall upon the moist humus of the woodland, new Ferns come forth from them. The propagation process is very intricate, it is true; it also takes a long time.

So while the higher plants lift their flowers up to the light, where the sun can wholly penetrate the pollen, and bees and butterflies carry it through the sun-filled air, the Ferns form their spores on the shady side of the fronds and let them fall without delay into the moist, dark soil. This shows us plainly that the sun has not yet wholly taken hold of these plants. They are still inclined toward the earth. If a flowering plant were to be developed out of a Fern, it would have to be turned upside down.

Scientists who have carefully investigated the petrified primeval Ferns have found them much more powerful and elaborate than ours of today. Many were developed into very tall Tree Ferns with giant fronds. Others flung themselves like tropical vines from tree to tree. Still others no longer tried to reach the ground beneath but remained high up in the crowns of the trees. Only in warm lands do Ferns today develop a similar luxuriance.

Primeval Ferns imitated flowering plants even more successfully than do ours of today. For example, many Ferns which formerly existed developed seeds—yes, veritable little fruits. But by the time the real flowering plants arose, the Ferns had forgotten how to form seeds.

The Horsetails (Equisetums)

The Horsetails are actually only skeletons. There are several kinds, most of them branched. Only a few grow as unbranched stems, and these look like bamboo canes. Not a single Horsetail can form leaves; they simply stand naked, as if their foliage had already fallen. If you wish to have a complete plant, therefore, you must add to the skeleton of the Horsetail the leaf of the Fern. But the Horsetails alone are only stem-parts. They take root much better in stony and sandy soil than do the Ferns, which need humus.

If you examine the Horsetails carefully, you notice that they are wonderfully divided even down to their finest twigs. At equal distances from one another there are always nodes (parts of the stem at which leaves and buds have their origin), and you can separate a Horsetail into as many parts as there are nodes.

    The side shoots, too, branch out only from the nodes. Since many branches spring forth from one node, a Horsetail is made up solely of several levels, each one like a story of a house, and each branching outward in the shape of a star. So when the Horsetails wish to imitate higher plants, they strive at each node to form flowers, but since they cannot succeed in this, they remain green and keep on growing. At the next node the same performance is repeated. Were the Horsetail a flowering plant, the side shoots would become petals or stamens. But it is only a Horsetail.

    Now what do these plants do when they want to produce their spores? They act quite differently from the Ferns. Since they are the purest stem plants, they imitate only the part of the flower that comes from the stem, namely, pistil and ovary. At the tip of the Horsetail sits the spore-case, which looks like a pine cone. It is a checkerboard, composed of many exact hexagonal shields. If you bend it, you can see that little white spore cases hang on the underside of the shields. Within these cases are the spores. Before a new Horsetail plant can arise from the spore, a much longer time is required than in the case of the Ferns—usually several years. The process is so troublesome.

The Field Horsetail has the most singular structure. It is often found as a weed in sandy fields. But it often appears also along railroad tracks, by the roadside and in building lots.

This Horsetail really takes on two different plant forms at different stages. As early as March thin brown stalks shoot forth. They are always unbranched and never green, for their chief task is simply to bear the spore cone. Then, when these brown, bruit-bearing stems have withered away, the green sprouts shoot up in the places where the brown ones stood. These are the true Horsetails. They remind one of small spruce or pine trees; they have little trunks and branches and a slender tip. It is, indeed, a strange thing that these green sprouts of the Field Horsetail produce no spore cones.

So we see that the brown, fruit-bearing stalks, together with the green, sterile ones which follow later, form one plant. They have, of course, a common rootstock deep down in the ground.

Often different plants must be joined together if all the elements of a complete plant are to be present. As we have already seen, the Fern and the Horsetail combined form a complete plant. Also, if the Fern leaf and the spore cone of the Equisetum could be united, then a flower would quite naturally result.

Many Horsetails growing together give the appearance of a little forest. If you shake them vigorously, they rustle, so much siliceous substance is contained in them. Formerly, the Horsetails were used to clean tinware, and so they came to be called Scouring Rushes.

In primeval times the Horsetails were much more important than they are today. Next to the Ferns, they formed a major part of the plant world.

If you want to picture to yourself how these primitive Horsetails looked, you must, above all, realize that they were very large. Some had trunks as high as 120 feet. They are, therefore, called Giant Horsetails. They had, however, no roots, but sprang out of other parts of trunks lying horizontally in the muddy ground. The side shoots were very profusely branched, so that a wood of Horsetails must have looked like an evergreen Coniferous forest.

The Club Mosses

There is little to say about Club Mosses, for in our present plant world they play only a very subordinate role. You see them now and then, especially in wood soil, creeping like snakes. Rarer kinds also form mats, out of short, upright shoots. They are covered over and over with little scale-like leaves and give the impression of being hairy. The name Lycopodium, by which the botanist calls them, means "wolf's foot." The spores, called "witch flour," are produced in little ears, which stand erect.

In primeval times of the earth the Club Mosses were trees many yards high, with powerful trunks projecting up into the air like telephone poles. Some bore tufts of ribbon-like leaves and formed crowns by forking repeatedly. If you consider these trees, the remains of which are also found in coal seams, you are very strangely impressed by them. They have been called Seal Trees and Scale Trees, because their trunks are marked closely with seal imprints arranged in oblique lines. These are the places where at one time leaves appeared (leaf scars).

The Seal Trees and Scale Trees were also more complete than our present Club Mosses, for plenty of cones hung from them, and so they were similar to our needle-bearing trees.

The Needle-bearing Trees (Conifers)

The main part of a Conifer is the trunk. Especially in very old Conifers, the woody part becomes stronger as time goes on. Since the cones turn to wood, you might say that in the Conifers even the fruits harden into wood.

The other parts, too, tend to contract, to harden. For example, you might think of the needles as leaves with only the midrib left. Between the deciduous trees—those which shed their leaves in winter—and the Conifers, there is a great difference, which is plainly recognizable in the outer form. A deciduous tree growing in a forest of Conifers stands out at once because of its altogether different way of branching, even when it has no leaves. The Conifers have high and unbranched trunks that stretch upward with side branches arranged like those of the Horsetails. This formation is especially clear in young trees. On the contrary, the trunk of a deciduous tree branches out like a network of veins, extending into the crown. Each tree has its special mode of branching.

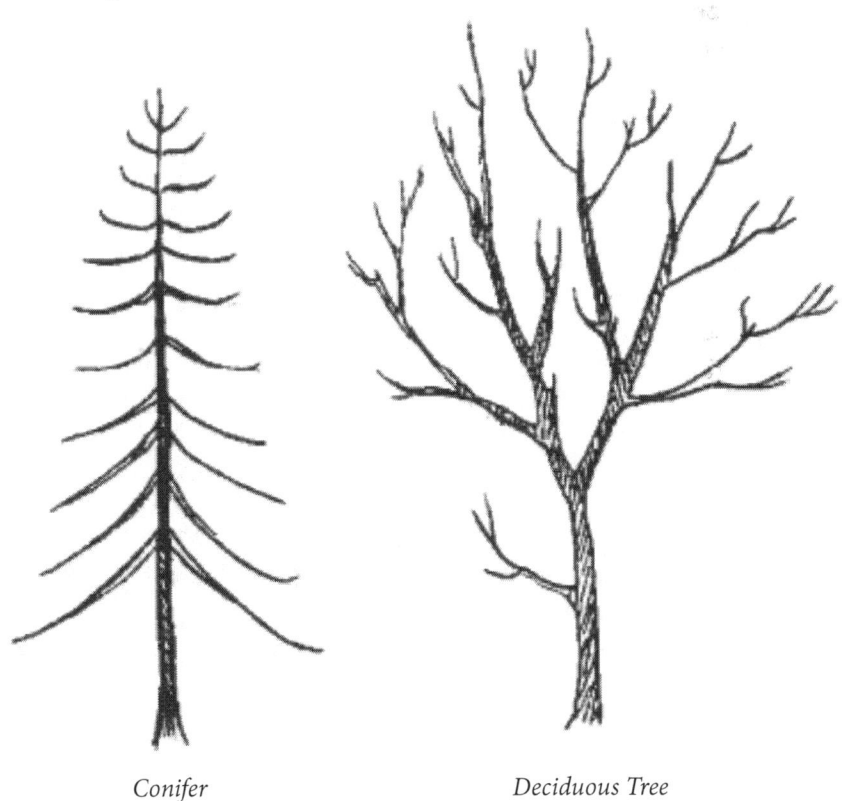

Conifer   *Deciduous Tree*

The name Conifer means cone-bearers. Each cone is a little tree. In the middle it has a tough axis, which might be called its little trunk. The scales are arranged around it in wonderful, regular, oblique lines, almost like the scales of fishes.

The cones are not only the fruits, but also the flowers of the Conifers (commonly called Evergreens). We have in the Evergreens, therefore, plants which cannot yet distinguish between flower and fruit. The flower becomes fruit when it simply becomes woody.

Take the Spruce as an example. In the blossoming time it forms two kinds of cones. The first, the real fruit cones, are at the start a beautiful crimson. They stand upright on the twigs and are less than a half an inch high. When they grow larger, they become green. Since they also grow heavier, they tilt over, so that later they hang downwards. Not until they ripen and become all wood do they turn brown.

The other cones, too—the much smaller pollen-cones—form in great numbers. If you shake them, the twigs give off pollen. There are years when the whole neighborhood is powdered with pollen dust. The Pine, especially, produces a great deal of pollen. It is called "sulfur rain." The pollen cones of the Spruce have short stems and remind one strongly of the spore cones of the Horsetails, which are of the same size. They are flesh-colored, and when they have spent their pollen, they fall from the tree. They are found then in great numbers, dried and dark brown, on the ground in the forest.

Since the Evergreens have no real flowers, but only scaly cones, they are visited by no insects when they bloom. (Insects visit them later on to extract the sweet juice from the needles.) The pollen is simply wafted by the wind and often is carried many miles.

The seeds of the Evergreens are also equipped for flying. Under each cone-scale are seated two seeds. They have wings which, if you examine them closely, remind you, not of butterflies, but at best of beetles' wings. If you take home a cone-bearing branch of Spruce and put it for a few days in a heated room, it dries out, and the scales spread apart. You should then hold it cautiously up high and shake it if you want to see a really amusing spectacle. From under the scales of the cone, hundreds of winged seeds whirl forth.

Scale of a spruce cone with two winged seeds.

If you compare the Conifers with the deciduous trees, you realize that the whole development of the Conifers moves very slowly. Their leaves never fall at the same time as those of other trees. The needles stay on the branches several years, and in some species a cone takes years to ripen. The Conifers grow very slowly. They possess great inner tranquillity. On entering an Evergreen forest, you are moved by a feeling of deep solemnity.

If a Conifer is injured, the aromatic resin drips out. It hardens in the air and becomes like amber. It is present in the wood as well as the bark, and even in the green cones; the whole tree is penetrated with it. It is because of the resin that the wood ignites so readily and burns with so bright a flame, as in the old-fashioned fire stick.

If you wonder how Conifers are able to produce these richly fragrant substances in trunk, bark, and needles, the answer is that the blossoming force has not been fully developed in these trees. The Conifers are really not wholly completed; otherwise, they would have true, fragrant flowers in place of their scaly cones. The flowers of the Conifer are hidden in the branches and needles, and the resin, as well as the volatile and inflammable oil, is nothing but transformed flower substance.

When a proper flowering tree unfolds, the blossoming force comes forth. You can observe it in actual forms and colors, and the fragrance streams into the open air. In the Conifers, whose life development moves too slowly, the flower-forming force is held back within the tree. It does not come freely to expression. Yet if you wish to make this force visible, you have but to kindle the wood or the brush. The clear, light-giving flame is the flower of the Conifer.

The insects, too, sense this secret. After warm summer days, when the Evergreen wood gives forth nectar, they can be heard humming and buzzing within it. Bees—yes, even butterflies—sip the sweet, flower-like juice which exudes from the dark needles. Pine honey is tarter than flower honey.

You understand the Conifers rightly only if you realize that the reason they have no flowers is that they do things too slowly. Before they arrive at the point of acting like the flowering trees, the wood-forming process has already overtaken them.

Two seedlings of a fir. Both seed leaves and first set of needles form a six-pointed star.

On the other hand, the Conifers are the first plants on the ladder of the vegetable kingdom to distinguish pollen from seeds. They form no spores, and for this reason are counted among the flowering plants. The formation of seeds is their best accomplishment, and on this account they should be called "seed plants."

Two Conifers—the Yew and the Juniper—even develop juicy fruits.

The Yew

The Yew has broad, soft needles, dark green on the upper side and light green below. It sheds its bark like the Plane trees. It has no cones, only red, berry-like fruits. Tall Yew trees are very scarce, for their growth is unusually slow and forests of Yew trees are a rarity. But in former times the Yew was very widely scattered. Loving the shade, and always held in high esteem by the Germanic tribes, it formed the undergrowth of the woods. The market place of the city of the gods, Asgard, was said to have been planted with Yews. Yew wood was especially suited for making the shaft of the bow. Today the Yews are about to die out. Only a few very old trees give evidence of the former glory of the Yew. The age of some specimens is estimated to be one or two thousand years. They sometimes attain a height of over thirty feet and a circumference of nine feet. Today the Yew is usually no more than a bushy growth. Its red fruits are not poisonous, but some animals become sick from eating the needles—horses, sheep, and goats, for example—although deer graze unharmed upon them. Yews are, unlike other Conifers, without resin, and they are dioecious. For this reason they occupy a very special place in the plant world.

The Spruce

This is the most important tree of our mountain woodlands. It is also called Red Fir, since its bark is rough and of a reddish color. The roots of the Spruce spread out flat like a plate; there is no taproot. When Spruces are uprooted by a storm, they tear out a mat of earth with them. The ripe Spruce cones hang downwards and fall off as a whole, in contrast to those of the White Fir, which remain upright and, still on the tree, unfold like the leaves of a book.

The Fir

This tree has a smooth, whitish-gray bark, and is also called the White Fir. Its needles form two rows on the stem and have two white stripes on the underside. Its cones stand upright and do not fall. A full-grown Fir can be distinguished at a glance from a Spruce because of the "eagle's nest" formed by the topmost branches.

The Pine

The needles of this tree are especially long, more than one of them—usually two—being bunched together. The crown is often umbrella-shaped, the cones short and made up of wedge-shaped, stout, woody scales. The Pine is the chief forest tree of the plains. It can grow in dry sand, in which it is held fast by its taproot. The Mountain Pine grows with its trunk and branches parallel to the ground. The Cembra Pine, or Siberian Pine, is also a tree of the high mountains. It has a thick trunk, and, compared with other Pines, still longer needles, which grow in graceful bunches. Pines from foreign countries are often planted because of their beauty, as, for example, the Weymouth Pines. Turpentine and rosin are obtained from the Pine.

The Larch

The Larch is the only one of our Conifers that sheds its leaves in winter. It extends far up the mountain slopes, where you often see little groups of these gleaming trees with their lofty trunks. The Larch is the Birch among the Conifers.

The Juniper

The trunk of this tree divides and branches thickly over the ground. The needles are hard and piercing. The Junipers form impenetrable thickets. They have no cones, only whitish-blue berries, which may be looked upon as merely transformed cones. They have an aromatic taste. The Juniper grows for the most part like a bush, standing alone. Many kinds of Junipers from foreign lands, spreading their crowns flat over the earth, are planted as ornamental shrubs. The Cypresses of southern countries are also Conifers, as well as the Arborvitae, often planted in churchyards. The Arborvitae has, however, no needles but only scale-like leaves. The small, woody cones prove, nevertheless, that it is a Conifer. The twigs of the Arborvitae have a fragrance, very like flowers.

The Families of the Flowering Plants

If you wish to distinguish and classify the flowering plants, you must learn how they are related to one another. Together they comprise a very large family. Some are as much alike as brothers and sisters; others are not so closely related. Plants show you their relationships most clearly when you examine and compare their flowers. You can learn much from their leaves, stems, roots, trunks, and fruits, also. For example, some relatives of the Clover have clover leaves. But here the distinctions are more difficult to understand, and you must have a great deal of experience if you would not err.

The large and manifold families of the flowering plants are further divided into sub-families. Each of them has a father and a mother, and the name "plant family" is used only in referring to these less pronounced relationships.

So, for example, the Rose has a family of its own. Its mother is the Rose; its father is the Apple Tree. Even a casual glance suffices to show the great similarity between the Apple blossom and the Wild Rose. The Raspberry, Blackberry, and Strawberry also belong to the plant family of the Roses. They stand between father and mother; the Strawberry is still a child.

Members of one and the same plant family have still other characteristics in common besides the flowers, as you see by the fact that the Raspberry and Blackberry produce woody stalks like the Rose. The thorns further indicate the relationship. At the same time it is apparent that you cannot judge by such marks alone, for the Strawberry is not a woody plant, and there are still other rose-like plants which do not grow like trees or bushes, but are merely herbs. On the other hand, there are many great trees which are by no means members of the Rose family.

Members of a single plant family, in spite of their relationship, sometimes behave very differently. Large and small, magnificent and modest, they occur side by side, as in a human family. The botanist draws the flowers, therefore, as they would appear if you observed them carefully from above. In the center of such a flower diagram, he draws the pistil. Around it are the stamens, and quite outside, the perianth, with petals and sepals. You can then see at once how the parts are arranged, how many there are, and which ones are missing. It makes no difference whether, for example, the petals are large or small, colored or only green, or whether they are transformed. Through the flower diagram you most easily recognize the relationships of the plants.

But naturally the flower diagram is only a help. The flower is certainly not the whole plant. He who wishes to understand a flowering plant rightly must observe much more than the number and arrangement of the parts of the flower. He must know what the plant does and how it behaves.

The Tulip and the Rose

Both of these are plants of remarkable beauty—splendid ornaments in our flower gardens. Though they are equally important for our enjoyment, yet in many ways they are absolutely different, even opposite from each other.

The first thing that occurs to us when we think of both these showy flowers is that the one—the Tulip—is a springtime plant, while the other—the Rose—does not bloom until summer. When the Rose blossoms begin to open, the Tulips have long since gone by, and at the time when our gardens are adorned with the gloriously colorful Tulip beds, hardly the first leaves are open on the Rose bushes.

The Tulip is a bulb plant. It has to be placed in the ground a year before it blossoms. What, really, is a Tulip bulb but a great, juicy bud! If you cut it through lengthwise and examine it with a magnifying glass, you make a remarkable discovery. In the heart of the Tulip bulb, the flower is already present in embryo; likewise, in a small, contracted form the plant leaves are there. Although all the parts appear only in a germ stage—the petals colorless, the stamens and pistil very indistinct—yet they are present. The stems need only to stretch out, the parts to enlarge, and the flower can unfold. It slumbers, enclosed in the sap-filled sheath of the bulb, the whole winter long.

How different it is with the Rose! If, as we have done with a Tulip bulb, we now examine the buds of the stalks from which the Rose sprouts, we find nothing resembling leaf scales—at most only the beginnings of the first foliage. Before the Rose forms its flower buds, it must have longer shoots, with beautifully formed leaves. And for all this, much time is needed, for the sun must work powerfully to bring it about.

Leaf of an apple tree

Leaves of a garden rose

Leaves of a wild rose

Where, then, in the Rose, you ask yourself, is that which corresponds with the bulb of the Tulip? Has the Rose such a part at all—or does it need none? The Rose does not possess a special bulb of its own, but it has something which serves it as the bulb serves the Tulip—only it is much larger and belongs to a great number of plants. In other words, the whole earth is its bulb! The sun must work very had to draw the Rose from the earth, so for this reason Roses do not bloom until summer.

Now it is quite clear that what takes so much longer to grow must be the more perfected. Just examine the leaves. In the Tulip they are simply broad, smooth-edged blades. They are never divided, nor have they any stem. But each leaf of the Rose is divided into parts, and where the stalk joins the branch there are again two little, pointed bracts. If you look at the edge of the leaf, you see that it is finely toothed. The Rose leaf is elaborated with a great deal of care. How much less carefully is a Tulip leaf formed! Finally, one cannot but think of a Rose as being very gracefully branched, while a Tulip stem always comes simple and undivided out of the ground.

The Tulip is in a great hurry when it bursts forth in the Spring. It wants to bring forth its flower as quickly as possible. So it takes no time to divide its parts carefully. The green foliage is just as simple as are the flower parts. Indeed, the Tulip does not even take the time to push its fruit out of the earth, for the bulb is at the same time its fruit, already formed the year before.

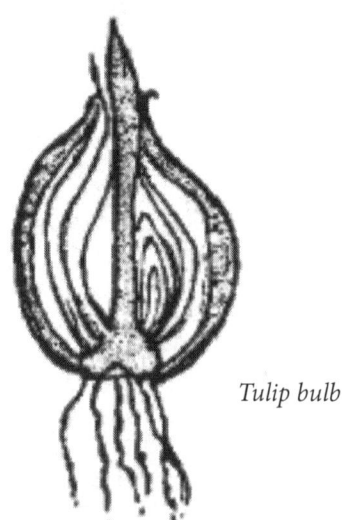

Tulip bulb

So you see that the flowers, leaves, and fruit of the Tulip are all mingled together. If you take a Tulip bulb apart, you learn that it is composed of a great number of fleshy leaf-scales.

The Tulip has no green calyx. Six petals, all alike, enclose the flower. In the Rose, on the other hand, five more green-fringed calyx tips appear under the colored petals. They enclose the flower bud until it unfolds. In the Tulip, calyx and corolla have become identical. The bud is at first green, and before it opens, its leaves simply develop color and become the flower petals. They are first calyx leaves (sepals) and then flower leaves (petals).

It often happens that the uppermost leaves of the Tulip stem acquire colored edges or that the petals remain half green. The transition to the flower is, indeed, likely to be blurred, since the whole process takes place so quickly.

But the Rose, which is often called the queen of the flowers, is quite a different plant! It comes forth slowly, taking a long time to divide calyx and corolla properly, until at last the fruit, the rose hip, develops from the blossom.

The Tulip is already withered at the time when the flower should ripen into fruit. It has spent all its strength, and instead of a fruit has only a dried-up seed vessel.

If you try to pull up a Wild Rose out of the ground, you will find how fast it is held. Under the earth is another inverted bush with many branches. The Rose is intimately bound up with the earth and lets the earth assist it. A Tulip bulb, on the other hand, is enclosed within itself. It holds onto the soil only with thread-like roots, which are never branched, but creep like worms into the earth. Is it any wonder that the Rose is able to form woody branches! It is capable even of developing into a little tree, for the earth force rises up above the ground with the Rose, endows it with wood and bark, and makes it enduring. When the Tulip has blossomed, it always has to withdraw quickly into its bulb. There it surrounds itself with a hard shell. So you can safely pull it up and store it when it is dried, or else force it to develop early, before it is warm enough to grow outdoors.

A six-pointed star is inscribed in the Tulip blossom; in the Rose, there is a five-pointed one, for the Tulip has six petals, the Rose only five, or—in the garden Roses—a multiple of five. The other parts also follow the same number pattern. So the Tulip has six stamens. To be more exact, you may actually say that they are twice three in number, for they stand in two triangles.

The Rose   The Tulip

Cross section through the triangular fruit knot (ovary) of the Tulip.

The pistil of the Tulip is formed also on a pattern of three. If you cut it across with a knife, you can see the cells into which it is divided. There are three, and the unripe seeds within are already visible. When the flower fades, the pistil is enlarged and becomes the seed vessel. The Rose has such a great number of stamens that it is not so easy to discover that they, too, are present in multiples of five. They stand side by side in thickly crowded circles and are vastly more delicate than those of the Tulip.

Again in the pistil of the Rose, sunk beneath the petals, and also again in the calyx, the simple number five is no longer to be found. But it is easily seen in the Apple, if one cuts it through crosswise.

Finally, there is one very important difference between the Tulip and the Rose. You must follow the leaf veins to find it. In the Tulip they are almost alike and run along side by side, so that a Tulip leaf looks striped. If it is torn, the fissures run lengthwise. Only in the tip of the leaf do the parallel veins come together. So you may describe the Tulip as a plant with parallel-veined leaves.

But if you try to tear a Rose leaf apart, the fissures run crisscross here and there, for the leaf veins of the Rose are branched, and their finest fibers run in and out like the arteries of man. Each leaflet has a midrib from which the side veins branch out. On examining the midrib, you find that the Rose has within it the strength to form a tree.

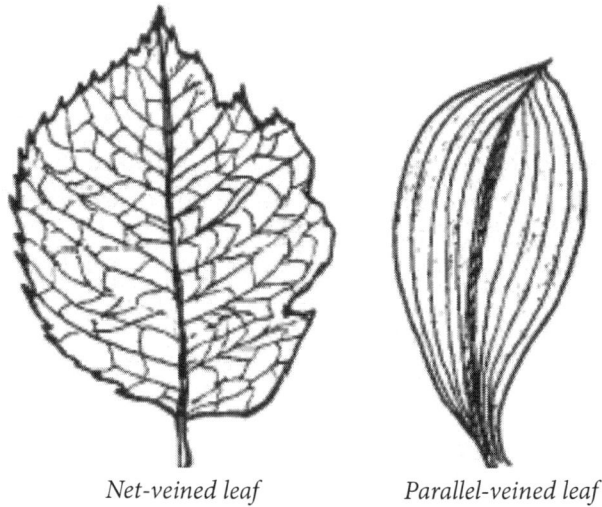

Net-veined leaf   *Parallel-veined leaf*

The Rose is described as a *net-veined* plant.

The kingdom of the flowering plants can be classified with respect to a plant's relation to the Tulip or the Rose. If it is similar to the Tulip, it is a parallel-veined plant, but if it is related to the Rose, it is a net-veined plant.

Parallel-veined and net-veined plants form the two great groups of the flower plant kingdom.

Summary of Some Characteristics of Parallel-veined and Net-veined Plants

Parallel-veined		*Net-veined*
Mostly formed on number three the Simple perianth (calyx and corolla)	Flowers	Mostly formed on the number five Double perianth (calyx and corolla)
Parallel-veined Never compound, without petiole and with smooth edges	Leaves	Net-veined Often compound or divided, with a petiole, and with toothed, sawed, or indented edges
Herbaceous, not woody, often simple	Stems	Often woody or simple with trunks forming branches and twigs
Often forming bulbs, tubers, or fleshy rootstocks	Roots	Never forming bulbs, but often shaving tough rootstocks
With only one seed-leaf, usually pointed (*Monocotyledons*)	Seedlings	Usually with two seed-leaves, often broad (*Dicotyledons*)

The Violet

The Violet, although so small, is one of the most beloved of plants. It may be so loved largely because it is among the first flowers to deck the land still gray after the flowerless time of the year. It even blooms as early as in March! But it has still other traits that endear it to us. Its flowers are so lovely and are so intensively colored that one color—violet blue—has been named from it and its perfume is strong and at the same time intimate.

(These qualities in the violet's perfume are not found so strongly in the American violet. Ed.)

The fact is that the Violet could not exist at all, if it were not so small. Its characteristics are contracted, as if to a point, and in this way strengthened.

Even before the flowers appear, you see the green leaves low on the ground. They are rolled up, funnel-shaped at first, like little listening ears. Although blooming so early, the Violet has no bulb nor other juicy parts like the Tulip, and it seems as if the fertile soil in which it is rooted had itself come to flower. This is due to the awakening sun of spring.

The Violet is a net-veined plant-therefore, a relative of the Rose, though in many respects unlike the Rose. The humpbacked, dwarfed flowers are not placed in the line of earth and sun. They open up sidewise and bend again towards the earth, for they are suspended on drooping stems. One of the petals protrudes backwards, so that a short spur, a nectar-bag, is formed. But how can the Violet, a relative of the Rose, bloom so early? How can it, without undue haste, form all its parts so carefully? How can its appearance be so lovely, its odor so sweet, its nectar so plentiful? Only because it is so small!

Poets best understand the Violet. They sense it even before it is present.

> Spring again leaves an azure veil
> Fluttering where the soft air flows—
> Sweet familiar fragrance blows
> Prophecy to hill and dale.
> Violets are dreaming
> Forth their urge to be.
> Hark! From far harp tones are gently streaming!
> It is thou, O Spring!
> I have witnessed thee!
> —Eduard Morike
> (Translated by Floyd McKnight)

The Violet is the earth's little flower-ear, which listens for these delicate tones. Botanists call it "Viola," which means violin. It belongs very intimately to the earth. She has drawn it close to herself and will not let it go.

The Violets spread abroad their flowers, very low over the earth, for the spring sun at first gives them no stalks, but only short flower stems. When the rootstock of the Violet has grown upward a little, its roots draw it back again. In this way the earth truly holds the Violet close to herself.

Later in the year it becomes very clear that the Violets cannot hold themselves up. The offshoots that they produce, seeking to spread out, run flat on the ground, almost like those of Strawberry plants. Since the Violets require so much strength in the spring when they bloom, they are exhausted later in the year and can only produce seedpods. Each seed contains a little nourishing appendage. This tidbit is especially for the ants, which help to spread the Violet over the earth's surface.

Since the Violet is not a large, fully-developed plant, and its flowers have to unfold down on the ground, it is not easily found; you must look for it a long time. (This refers to the European Violet.) But it likes to be discovered. With eager expectation it peeps forth from its green leaves. Only a number of Violets together really make any kind of a display, and you have to bind many of them to form a really sizable bunch.

The Pansy is closely related to the Violet. It is larger, and instead of being merely a little ear, it is a whole face, with an especially beautiful skin. The Pansy is a larger plant, with more green parts than the Violet, and it has a longer stem. The leaf force, which in the Violet forms the green foliage, has gone into the blossom of the Pansy. This metamorphosis appears less pronounced in the wild Pansy but shows itself more clearly in the many-colored petals of the garden Pansy's flowers.

The Buttercup

When the yellow Buttercups are in bloom, the meadows are at their loveliest. You can pick fragrant bunches of various flowers in which no color is wanting. And how luminous and delicate they all are! Especially when there are Bluebells nearby, the rich yellow contrasts gloriously with the blue and violet.

There are many varieties of Buttercups, and this flower is found in areas far removed from one another. With few exceptions—one of which is the White Water Buttercup, or Crowfoot—all varieties of Buttercup are similar, having yolk-yellow flowers. The most important and familiar among them is the common Buttercup of the meadows. It has its scientific name (Ranunculus Acer) from its sharp taste.

The leaves of the sharp Buttercup are palmately lobed, with pointed tips, and actually remind one of hen's feet. The leaf surfaces, also, are often decorated with dark brown markings.

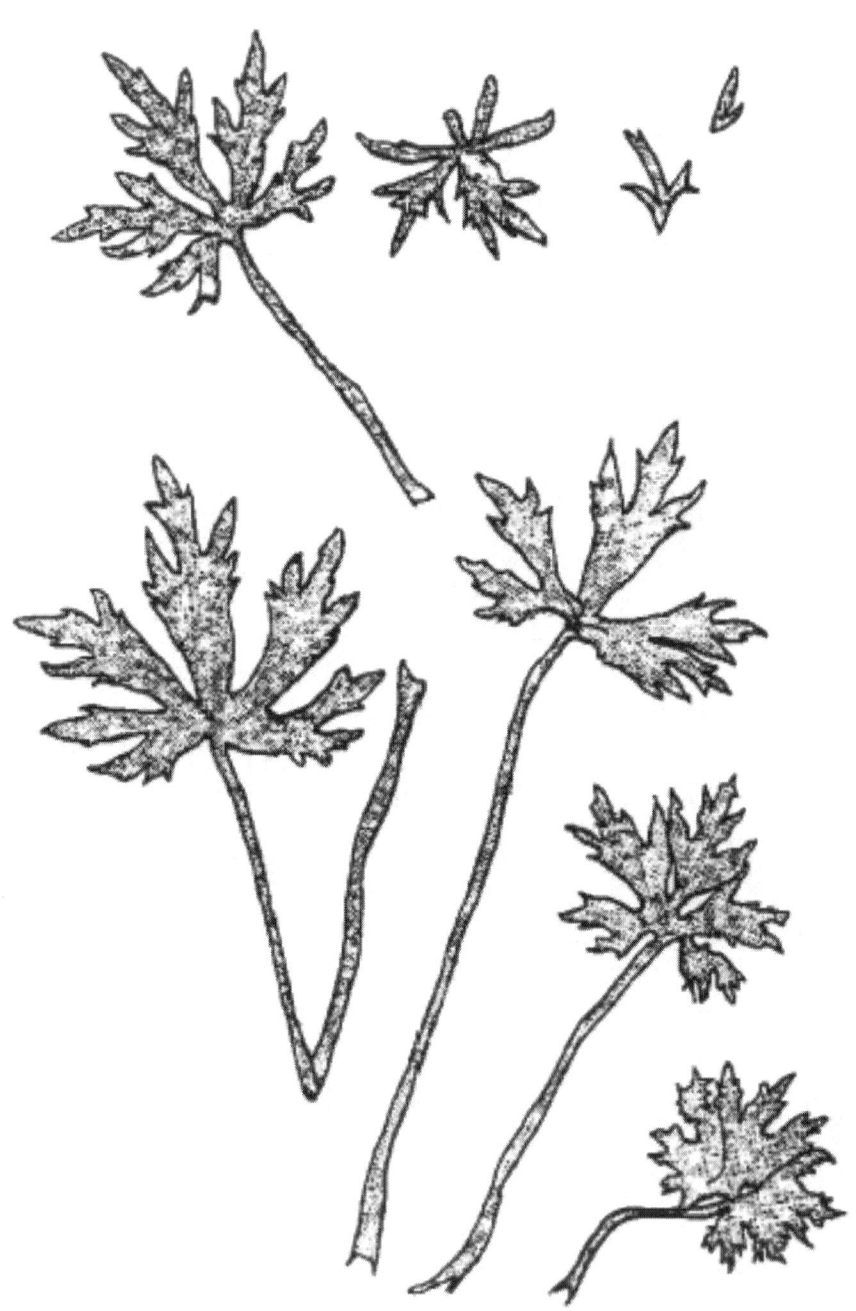

Gradual leaf metamorphosis of Ranunculus acer.

The Buttercup has a long, slender stem, branched at the top. The sun has shaped it so as to kindle at last the little light of the yellow flower. If the single blossom is not so important as that of the Poppy, for Buttercup blossoms are much smaller—yet so many of them grow together that they color the meadows yellow far and wide. Especially when you see such a meadow from afar, you realize that it is not the single flower that counts, but the whole mass. The earth itself wishes to flower at this season.

But one can study in the single plant how the sunlight acts when it takes hold of the earth, changing and shaping it.

The lowest leaves are the broadest, and in spite of their pointed tips, the surfaces have grown together on their long stalks. If, then, you follow the leaves of a Buttercup plant further up the stalk, you see that the leaf stem (petiole) becomes shorter. At the same time the leaf tips become smaller. The leaf becomes, in general, much simpler. The uppermost leaves—those nearest to the blossoms—are especially small. They have no petiole at all, and the few tips which compose them are narrow, with smooth edges (entire). Finally there is only a single ray left; petiole and leaf surface have become united.

If you did not know that the uppermost and lowest leaves grew on the same plant, you would never believe that they belong together. But if you give more careful thought to the matter, you discover that the simple upper leaves are comparable to the parts of which the lower ones are composed, so that you have an upper leaf, if you tear off a piece of an under one.

The reason why the under leaves are more enlarged is that there is more moisture in the neighborhood of the earth. In all moist regions the leaves become larger and more luxurious than in dryer places, as may be observed in many plants.

Particularly is the Marsh Marigold, a sister of the Buttercup, a case in point. Standing by the brookside, it grows thick and fleshy, and its leaves, although excessively healthy, remain coarse and undivided. Finally, the light adds to it an indented edge. The Marsh Marigold grows so riotously that it gets too heavy and has to lie flat on the ground.

You may also notice the blossom of the Marsh Marigold—how weak it is in spite of its luxuriance. It is gloriously yellow, it is true, but it has only a simple perianth, while the Buttercup has a double one. The green sepals of the Marsh Marigold bud are transformed into petals by the spring sunlight. So easily does this flower take life that it spares itself the trouble of forming special green sepals.

But the Buttercup is no such lazy fellow. It shoots right up in the air, splits its stalk into slender offshoots, and branches in the open air. Before the flowers come, the green foliage recedes, step by step, from the top downwards. At last all is so well prepared that the sun can place the delicate flower lightly on the tip of the stalk. Each flower has five shining, yellow petals, with a greenish calyx in five parts.

Were the Buttercup not mowed down, it would dry up soon after flowering; for as great an artist as is the Buttercup in the transformation of its leaves, its upper parts are not lasting. When the yellow flowers fall, only the little dried, spiky bunches stretch upwards. These are the seedpods which have developed from the pistils, standing in the center of the Buttercup blossom.

The Buttercup is a plant which easily and very willingly transforms its leaves. If you compare the different varieties carefully, you are greatly astonished at their power to produce many forms. This is one of the most fascinating studies of a botanist.

Sudden leaf metamorphosis of the golden-yellow Buttercup

The relatives of the Buttercup—the Crowfoot family—carry over this great power of transformation even to the flower parts. In fact, you no longer know whether a part now is calyx, corolla, or stamen, for all interplay with one another.

Thus, plants arise—as the Monkshood and the Larkspur—whose relationship to the Buttercup family is easily recognized in their green leaves.

The Stinging Nettle

The Nettle is a strong—and at the same time a beneficent—plant. Although it makes no show of itself externally, yet it is worthy of respect. Whenever man has disfigured the earth, it comes and covers the spot with its dark green. It is often found in dump heaps. It penetrates the soil with its creepers, which send leaf sprouts upwards.

The Nettle is a plant which thrives best near human beings, for there it finds most to do. It follows man to the loneliest mountain huts, and even long-forsaken human habitations can be discovered by the Nettles growing round about. The Nettle grows in all ruins and around abandoned camp sites. In open nature it is much rarer.

Even in the worst soil this plant has healthy, beautifully-formed leaf shoots. The stately plant often forms bushes as high as a man, so thick that no other plant finds room to grow between them. No one should treat a Nettle badly because it is only a Nettle. It does, indeed, compensate for a great deal of harm that man has done. From young Nettles gathered in the spring you can make soup. Its strength then goes over into the blood and purifies it even as the growing plant purifies the impure soil. It could never work so powerfully upon men and earth if it did not have in it so much fire.

You need quietly examine a Nettle only once to discover how beautiful it actually is. Its leaves are arranged in four rows. Two leaves appear opposite each other, and the following pair forms a cross with the preceding. If you look at a Nettle from above, you very plainly see the leaf arrangement in four rows. Each leaf is drawn out to a point, with the edge sharply indented. A glance at these leaves immediately gives warning to beware. The Nettle is provided with fine, glass-like bristles called Nettle-hairs. If you touch them, they break off and pierce the skin, so that the biting juice may flow into the little wound. Pain results, but otherwise no harm is done. In foreign lands there are Nettles which poison, while at the same time they bum; ours, however, have only a harmless fire.

The stalk of the Nettle has four sharp edges. It does not form wood, but only coarse fibers. If you cut an old Nettle stalk here and there and rub it, the outer layers gradually come off and the fibers appear. They can be twisted into a thread. In former times the Nettle was extensively cultivated, and its fibers were spun and woven, for Nettle cloth is a very good material.

Having become large and stately, the Nettle sets out to bloom. But how inconspicuous are its flowers! Since a Nettle is a wind-pollinated flower, it has no color or petals, no perfume or nectar. It would not suit the Nettle to appear outwardly beautiful and striking, so it will not waste its strength in flowers, for the best part of this plant is under the ground, where it so prepares the soil that other plants less strong can grow there. So it is not at all a weakness that the Nettle—in place of beautiful flowers—allows only inconspicuous, greenish catkins to hang at different heights from its stem. The Nettle, like the Willow, is a dioecious plant. Some Nettles produce only staminate blossoms, others only pistillate; both types grow catkins.

The bees and the butterflies, of course, do not care at all about the Nettle flowers, which offer them no nectar. If you stand in front of a flowering Nettle bush in the morning hours, you may witness a curious performance. From time to time, after a minute explosion, a little cloud of pollen flies up. The stamens of the Nettle burst with a jerk and fling their dust-dry pollen into the air. You may take a Nettle indoors, if you wish to observe the pollen to better advantage.

One who really understands the Nettle knows that it has to be so inconspicuous, since all its strength turns inward. Its blossom-force has become Nettle-force and remains in the green leaves. The Nettle gives the appearance of a plant not yet completed, and just when you think the colorful blossoms are coming forth, its growth is already at an end.

But it is clear that the force that stays in the leaves is in reality the blossom-force held back. The Nettle itself has no flower, but it nourishes the caterpillars of butterflies. Two of our most beautiful butterflies—the Peacock and the Small Tortoise-Shell—lay their eggs in the Nettle. When the caterpillars devour the leaves, they take into themselves the fiery blossom-force. They change into the chrysalis form when they have grown large enough, and after the chrysalis stage the gaily colored butterfly emerges.

The Peacock and the Small Tortoise-Shell butterflies are the Nettle's flowers, flying about in the air. True, they have not grown on the plant, but none the less they belong to it, for the Nettle has given up its fire-force to the caterpillars, which have then further transformed it. The chrysalis of the butterfly is also the Nettle's flower bud, and the butterfly can carry further what the Nettle has held back.

The Nettle reminds one of those people who, unnoticed by anyone, are always doing good. They are, like the Nettle, possibly even disregarded and misunderstood, because they seek no renown and no position. But if you consider what they bestow upon other human beings, then you recognize how worthy of reverence they are.

The Dead Nettle

The Dead Nettle is very similar to the Nettle in the manner in which its green shoots are built, but it is in reality a wholly different plant. It is a *Dead* Nettle; that means it does not sting.

The Dead Nettle and the Nettle are found in similar places. They thrive well near garden fences or damp walls. In other words, they love shade and coolness. Although the Dead Nettle does not actually seek out the woodland twilight, yet it avoids those places where the sun scorches unmercifully. Above all things this plant likes moist ground, in which its creeping stalk parts can luxuriate.

The Stinging Nettle feels quite at home in the hot sun and would gladly be made to glow by its rays; the Dead Nettle, on the contrary, stands the drought and intense heat less well. For this reason the spring is its best flowering time. If exposed to drought or strong light, it does not grow larger, but it actually gets smaller. Its sprouts draw back again into themselves.

The Dead Nettle might also be called the "Mild" or "tender" Nettle. Even the leaves show that it has in it no such fire as the Nettle has.

The stalks of the Dead Nettle are four-edged, like those of the Nettle. The position of the leaves also is the same in both plants. But in the flowers the contrast between the two becomes obvious. The Nettle is a wind-pollinated flower, but the Dead Nettle is pollinated by the bumblebee.

Everyone knows the white blossoms of the Dead Nettle (in this country the Dead Nettle has purple flowers), for the whole flower looks like a wide-opened jaw. There is also an underlip, and on the left and right there are two little teeth. The Dead Nettle blossom is so radically transformed that you scarcely realize it is made up of five petals which have grown together. Botanists have, nevertheless, proved this.

The Dead Nettle is, thus, clearly a net-veined plant, though, of course, completely unlike the Rose.

If you pick a Dead Nettle flower, you can suck out the sweet nectar collected in the inner flower tube. The bumblebees consider the Dead Nettle flowers as their honey pots. Without the bumblebees this flower could not be understood at all, for it has truly been formed only for them.

Since the Dead Nettle is more moist and cooler than the Nettle, the blossom-force does not remain in the leaves, but surges out at the top. The consequence is that flowers are produced by the Dead Nettle. They are mild and soft like the whole plant and long for the bumblebees, which come flying from the side. These flowers would like to enclose the bumblebees and adjust their form to these insects as completely as possible.

The roof of the Dead Nettle flower is formed for the back of the bumblebee. Stamens and pistil are so placed that the sucking bumblebee must touch the anther and the stigma. The inner flower tube admits the head and the outstretched tongue of the bumblebee, and the underlip of the Dead Nettle stands so that the bumblebee can clasp it comfortably while it sucks.

You see, therefore, that the Dead Nettle flower has actually succeeded in forming an exact cast of the bumblebee's body. Thus, the plant longs for the insect and reaches out toward it.

After the blossom force of the Dead Nettle surges up, a mild, non-fiery Nettle must naturally remain behind. The bumblebee belongs to the Dead Nettle exactly as does the gaily colored butterfly to the Nettle. It is its freely-moving other half. One may imagine that the hairs which the Dead Nettle should properly possess have, in the transformation, gone over to the insect and grown fast to the back of the bumblebee. They have become the sting of the insect and fly about with it in the air.

Thus, you see, just as in Nettle and butterfly, so in Dead Nettle and bumblebee, the insects are a continuation, as it were, of the plants.

THE RELATIVES OF THE DEAD NETTLE

All plants formed like the Dead Nettle are called Labiates. The Dead Nettle is the mother of this plant family (commonly known as the Mint Family); the father is the Rosemary shrub, which grows in the warm Mediterranean countries.

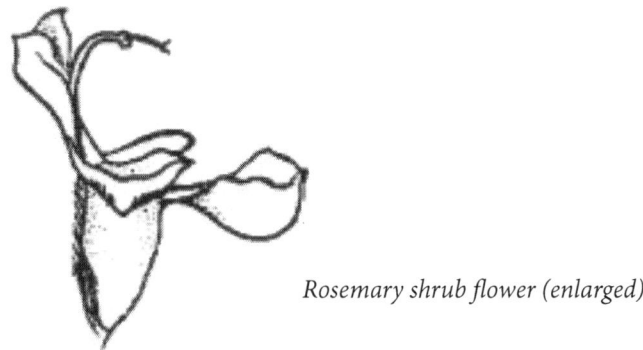

Rosemary shrub flower (enlarged)

Many Labiates are low, even dwarf-like, shrubs with small flowers and leaves. Just think, for instance, of the Thyme plant. Small as it is, it has woody stalk parts, and so must be considered a dwarf bush. When its rosy bloom appears in midsummer on the sunny hillsides, there is everywhere a humming and buzzing about one's ears. Many bees swarm through the warm air, which is filled with a sweet, etheric fragrance.

Since these Labiates grow in the hot sun, they are warmed throughout much more intensely than other plants. The sun penetrates deep into the leaves and forms within them a fine fragrant oil. So, of course, the flowers must remain small. The blossom force is pressed back by the sun into the green parts of the plant. So it comes about that both leaves and stalk are fragrant. The Dead Nettle, you will notice, has larger flowers, but its perfume is weaker. It is musty, for the Dead Nettle flourishes generally in moist places.

The plant family of the Labiates is divisible, on the one hand, into those species which are more similar to the Dead Nettle, and, next to them, those which grow more in the sun and in dry places. These have smaller flowers but more fragrant leaves. Balm, Mint and Peppermint must be grouped on this side.

White Dead Nettle	*Rosemary*
Spotted Dead Nettle	Lavender
Yellow Dead Nettle	Garden Sage
Small Dead Nettle	Thyme
Prunella	Hyssop
Ground Ivy	Marjoram
Bugle (Ajuga)	Savory
Meadow Sage	Oregano
Hedge Nettle	Basil
Hemp Nettle	Peppermint
Germander	Lemon Balm

Even if you do not know all the plants named here, you will, nevertheless, see from this summary that the Labiate flowers include many valuable aromatic herbs and important medicinal plants. Those which are most valuable to man grow in the sunlight, or are at least very strongly penetrated by the sun's rays. They can then carry over the sun force for mankind to use when it is needed.

The Bird Vetch (Bird's Tare)

The Vetches are plants which cannot be imagined apart from other plants. They always need outside supports upon which to climb. When Bird Vetch (Bird's Tare) grows in grain fields, as it so often does, its curly tendrils seize now this stalk, now that. These tendrils feel about them like one who, in sleep, half dreaming, gropes for an object, although, of course, they do this without any consciousness of what they do. If these tendrils could find no support, they would remain lying pitifully on the ground.

So the Bird's Tare grows in the open spaces between other plants. It is not a climbing plant, for its stalk does not twine about other plants as does the Bindweed, but hangs from them and sways freely, since it fastens itself around them. The curling tendrils are hands with which the Bird's Tare makes secure its airy existence. You feel that it would laugh if it could, for it is a jolly fellow!

The Bird's Tare shows us what happens if the air gets the upper hand in a plant. It is truly an example of a plant that has acquired its agility and movement from the air. If it stood more firmly on the earth, it would doubtless have a more rigid stalk, but, as it is, if you tear it away from its entanglements and hold it freely, it just hangs down loosely.

The leaf of the Bird's Tare is profusely feathered (pinnate). On the left and right of the midrib are many pairs of leaflets. Each has a short stemlet which is at the same time like a joint. So the little leaf can turn about easily, as the leaflets of the Bird's Tare must often do. Sometimes they stand rigidly erect; sometimes they spread out flat; again they droop downwards. Their relation to light and their stage of development determine their position. How great must be the sensitivity of this plant, that each of its many little leaflets can move by itself!

At the tip of the leaf the little leaflets are transformed into tendrils, which are most aptly described as feelers. The midrib, also, extends into such a feeler.

At first the feelers are greatly elongated, delicate, and soft. They feel about all around them. Then, if they touch a firm object, the tendrils bend and curl themselves securely around it for support. If they do not find such support, then they simply curl themselves up like snails.

The blue-violet flowers of the Bird Vetch, arranged in the form of little spikes, all facing in one direction, look like a flock of birds. Many of these flowers grow together, so each single flower is small.

If you examine the parts of a Vetch flower, you are reminded of the air. The names which the single little petals bear are taken from objects which move in the air. The largest petal, standing upright in the center of the flower and forming, so to say, its face, is called the *flag*. To the left and right extend two more petals, called *wings*, and the two lower ones, growing together in the form of a beak or canoe, are called a little *boat*. The sides of the little boat enclose ten stamens and the ovary, style, and stigma.

Birds Tare

Finally, the Vetch may be compared with the Rose, to which it is related, for it is also a net-veined plant. Like the Rose it has a five-parted flower as well as a calyx. The pinnate leaves also show the relationship between these flowers.

The Rose finds support in itself; the Vetch has to seek it elsewhere. This difference results from the fact that the Rose is lifted out of the earth by the sun, while the Vetch is formed mainly by the air. The Bird

Vetch is rooted in the ground, it is true, but the earth-force does not rise up with it.

When the Roses have fallen, sun and earth bring forth a second great miracle. You might say that the Rose blooms a second time when its fruits and the scarlet hips ripen. The flowers of the Bird Vetch simply become flat green husks (pods). Only the birds feed upon their seeds, hence, the name "Bird Vetch" (or "Bird's Tare").

The blossoms of the Rose are placed in the line of earth and sun, but those of the Bird Vetch look sidewise like little birds. A blossom formed like that of the Bird Vetch is called a "butterfly" (papilionaceous) flower, but it might be more aptly called a "bird blossom."

When the flowering time is past, the petals become discolored as if a little bird had died.

The Grasses

All the flowers and herbs, trees and shrubs would not suffice fully to clothe the body of the earth; the grass—the turf—must stretch over it and cover its nakedness, like the fur of an animal. Each blade of grass sprouting forth is the answer of the earth to a ray of sunlight. If you wish to draw a picture of grass, simple strokes pointing from the earth to the sun are sufficient. For grass never has broad surfaces; the force of the stem dominates everything.

It is especially noteworthy that the grasses have no true flowers. On their slender blades they rock their panicles and ears happily in the wind, but no one has ever seen a grass blade which bore a colorful flower, be it ever so small. A deep secret of nature lies hidden in this peculiarity.

As long as the grasses have only leaves, they all look alike. Not until they produce their panicles and ears do they show that there is an extraordinary number of different kinds.

Various Grasses

A stalk of grass has as many leaves as it has nodes, for a node is the place on the stalk where a leaf sprouts. The grass leaf, however, does not at once sprout off sidewise, but is wrapped first around the stalk for a space. In this way the leaf sheath is formed. From this it is evident that the leaves of the grasses also are ruled by the force of the stalk. They have to follow the stalk first before they are able to turn sidewise. If you pull a leaf of grass, it does not tear away at the place where it seems to sprout, but you rip down the tubular leaf-sheath, which you had not noticed at first. The sheath often forms the largest part of the leaf. Within the sheath the grass stalk has kept soft and juicy. It is most delicate directly over the node, where it is most easily torn asunder when pulled.

The wonderful, finely-divided panicles and ears are likewise composed of pure stalk parts. Often their little branches stretch far into the air; sometimes, also, they are contracted into bundles or rollers, as in the Meadow Foxtail. Each kind of grass behaves differently. Grass is indestructible. It grows throughout the year without care, quickly covering over any bare spot that appears.

Only because it remains flowerless does grass possess this great force of life and growth. For this reason it is never weary but stays ever young and fresh. When the meadows are mowed down, it begins right away to sprout forth again from its rootstocks. Far and wide through the soil creep the underground runners of the Couch Grass. If you want to uproot them, you have to dig up the ground and carefully pick them out; otherwise, all is soon green again.

The sun sends into the earth with its rays a very powerful force when it produces grass, a force great enough to bring into being many splendid flowers. But the earth does not wish flowers to grow on grass stalks; she prefers to leave them undeveloped.

The leaves of grass are so slender and pointed that they can hardly be called leaves, for in order to be leaves, they should have broad, juicy surfaces and become more like herbs. The earth holds the leaves of grass back in herself, allowing only the parts that are stem-like to sprout.

So it is no wonder that the panicles and ears of the grasses are made up of only delicate stalk parts. In reality they are blossom stems, all of which would like to have flowers. But the earth holds them in herself; they are allowed nothing but stems. Only stamens—attached to delicate threads—and pistils are formed, whose stigmas look like tiny little feathers. Otherwise, the "grass flowers" consist only of beards. They are the undeveloped flower-calyx.

It is quite obvious that the earth, providing no real flowers for the grasses, must look after the pollination, for neither bees nor butterflies visit the "grass flowers." She leaves everything to the wind. It wafts the pollen. The grasses are wind-pollinated plants (anemophilous). It is only because the earth gives no flowers to the grasses that they can become so valuable to mankind. What would we eat if the grasses should adorn themselves—if they were not forbidden to develop the loveliest part of plant life, the flower? They have to renounce this. All our grains—wheat, rye, barley, oats, corn, rice, and sugarcane—are varieties of grasses.

How grateful should mankind be to the earth for producing plants that do not waste their fruitfulness in outer beauty, but cherish it that we may be nourished!

For the fruit of the grain is only a seed. All the unspent strength of the grain plant goes into it. It stores up its life within the seed, as in a little treasure box. And what strength the sun adds to it until, through the many summer days, the corn ripens and the ears grow brown. It is a true gift of sun and earth—this yearly harvest of grain—and man should reverently think of it and reverently partake of his daily bread.

A Blessing before Meals
Earth, who gave us this food;
Sun, who made it ripe and good;
Dearest Earth and Dearest Sun,
We'll not forget what you have done.
—Christian Morgenstern

We eat bread and take the nourishing force of the grain seed into our blood. But there it is changed. The strength of the grain finally comes to flower—becomes like red roses. Man has this strength in his blood; otherwise, he could not be a man. The nobler and purer a man is, the more beautiful are the roses in his blood. These cannot be seen with the physical eyes, it is true; even so, they are present.

It is the same with the grain seed. You can give it back to the earth and sow it. Then the earth's body comes to fruit with the indwelling sun forces. A new grain plant comes forth from the seed. Instead of sowing it, you may eat it in bread. Thus transformed, it blooms in man's blood. Blood and bloom are related words. Then the grain fructifies the soul and strengthens it for good deeds.

Finally, we should bring to mind the simple grasses which the cattle find in the meadow or which are laid in the manger as hay. They, too, are transformed to become milk or meat, which also serve us as nourishment.

This is the great secret which lies enclosed within the flowerlessness of the grasses.

If the grains were to bring forth flowers, we should have no bread. But the earth decks the fields of grain in another way. She strews the Cornflowers, Corn-cockles, Poppies, and many other flowers among the grains. Through weeds the grain field is given something which it would otherwise be denied. This is the goal toward which the earth strives—to balance all that is one-sided and never to let beauty fail.

The Cabbage and its Relatives

The Cabbage plant is an artist who can perform a thousand tricks. You hardly know what it really looks like, for before it has had time to complete its development, man has eaten it up.

For in one particular way the Cabbage plant is remarkably gifted: it allows itself to be fattened. That alone would perhaps not be at all unusual, for you can do likewise with a Pumpkin. But if a plant succeeds in fattening all conceivable parts but those where you would expect it (in the fruit), you must regard this as most unusual.

But how would a Cabbage plant look if it could develop normally? Incredible though it seems, it is by nature a slender plant. It has a long, powerful stem, with luxurious, often pinnated leaves. The Cabbage stem is continued below in the taproot; above it extends into the flower heads.

You often see Cabbage blooming in the country, where it is planted for the seed that it yields. It sprouts there in the second year, and the flower stem breaks through. Its flowers are sulfur-yellow. Since they have four petals arranged in the form of a cross, they are called *Cruciferous* blossoms, and all the almost countless relatives of the Cabbage are designated as the family of the Cruciferous plants (commonly known as the Mustard family).

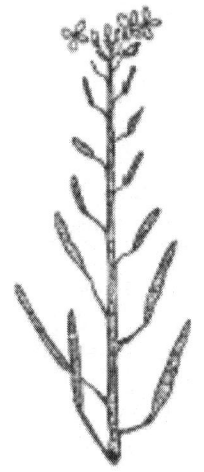

Inflorence of Mustard family (Crucifer)

A Cruciferous plant is very easily recognized. One needs but to examine its flower stem, especially when it is somewhat lengthened, for it grows and blooms further and further at the tip. The older blossoms form their pods, which are spread out on every side like the candles on a branched candlestick. Sometimes there is an enormous number of them, filling the flower stem from bottom to top. When you realize that a great many seeds are arranged in each pod, you can imagine what a quantity of seeds a single Cabbage plant brings forth.

This is the other side of Cruciferous flowers—that they have an enormously strong seed-force. Some produce seeds like the sand on the seashore and spread out so profusely that they become troublesome weeds. The Charlock and its cousins are the commonest weeds of the fields. Some Cruciferous plants also have shorter and broader pods, for example, the Shepherd's Purse and Pennywort.

But what a remarkable plant the Cabbage must be, that man has been able to develop it so as to send the force of propagation into the leaves and stems and to make them fat! Our different varieties of Cabbages have arisen because the growth force was held back at some point of development—at a different place in each kind of Cabbage. You can count up the parts of a plant and consider in each case what sort of Cabbage must arise if the growth force is guided into this part.

If the taproot is large and strong, you have the Rutabaga, but if the stem above the ground is thickened, the result is the droll Kohlrabi, upon which the leaves grow as on a proper stem. You can even see how they are arranged in a spiral line.

If the growth force of the Cabbage plant goes into leaves, we have the green Cabbage, which must first be frozen in order to taste good. But if the bud at the end of the stem is developed to enormous size, the resulting plant is a head Cabbage—white, red, or Savoy.

But the possibilities are still not exhausted with all these variations. In the axis of its leaves, on the stem, are the buds from which the side shoots can sprout forth when the plant wants to branch. If, now, the growth force goes into these buds at the leaf axis, so that they form little leaves which fold together like miniature Cabbage heads, then

Brussels Sprouts develop (called in German *Rosenköhl*, "Rose Cabbage"). It is named after the Rose, since the little Cabbage roses have the form of flowers.

You might perhaps think there were no further possibilities of transformation, but one still remains to be mentioned—the Cauliflower. It comes into being when the flower head becomes fat and fleshy, instead of stretching out and becoming long. Then it forms ever so many more shoots. You can see plainly on the surface of a Cauliflower the single flower buds. If a Cauliflower is not cut off at the right time, it shoots up finally, comes fully into the light, and forms a profusely branched, flowering bush. To prevent this, the green Cabbage leaves must be bent inward until they cover the Cauliflower, so that no sunlight can shine upon it. It then remains pale and fleshy.

Inflorescence	▸	Cauliflower
Stems	▸	Kohlrabi
Leaves	▸	Green Cabbage
Buds	▸	Brussels Sprouts
Stem buds	▸	Head Cabbage
Taproot	▸	Rutabaga

When the varieties of Cabbage are enumerated, not quite all of the useful plants of the Cruciferous family are named. Winter Radishes and the Common Radish also are brothers of the Cabbage plant. In these plants, as in the Kohlrabi, the taproot is overdeveloped.

Other Cruciferous plants, also, are cultivated for their seeds. Rape is raised in the fields, because its seeds contain a valuable oil. The Mustard seed also produces an oil—mustard oil—which is noted for its sharp taste.

Many Cruciferous plants have sulfur-yellow flowers. Fields of Rape are recognized from afar by their raying yellow, but fields abounding in Charlock and Wild Mustard also impress the eye pleasantly, at least through their shining color.

The sulfur force shows itself especially in the color of the flowers of those Cruciferous plants in which it is not in any way inwardly consumed. Thus, the Mustard plant, with its sharp-tasting seeds, has only white blossoms. So have the winter and common Radish. But the milder Rape shines with a sulfur-yellow.

As red-hot iron loses its heat when dipped in cold water, so in the fleshy-growing, watery Cabbage plant the sulfur-force is present, but in a weakened form.

Some Cruciferous flowers act very differently from the useful plants or field weeds mentioned thus far. They prefer fragrant blossoms. Wallflower and Stock (Gilliflower) are, for example, among our most beautiful ornamental plants. If you should wish to enumerate all of them, you would have to call to mind, also, the many "cushion" plants of the Cruciferous family, cultivated in rock gardens, with violet-blue and yellow blossoms and also the white Wall-cress. These ornamental plants have, of course, no importance for man's nourishment.

Bouncing Bet also spends its forces in producing a larger and more beautiful flower than most of the other members of this family and so can be of no practical use.

The Dandelion

This plant is well-known to all children, not only for its splendid, raying, sun-like blossoms, but because many kinds of chains, sucking straws, and other things can be made from its stems.

Dandelion flowers appear in the spring. Somewhat later they have turned into white lanterns, or, as some say, into "blow flowers," for when you blow one of these flowers, many parachutes fly merrily off. They are the tiny fruits of the Dandelion. Beneath each parachute hangs a very small seed.

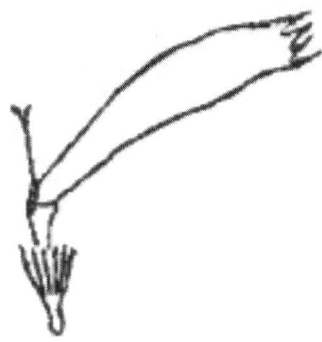

Flower head with one parachute left *Closed flower head* *Single ray flower of dandelion*

Gardeners love the Dandelion less than the children do, for it often grows where it is not wanted at all and spreads far and wide, and no one knows whence it comes. Of course, it is brought by Brother Wind, who carries the parachutes along. If you pull up a Dandelion plant, you generally have in your hand only the leaves. The taproot, which reaches deep into the soil, is held fast. So you accomplish nothing without the help of a spade. If the root, leaves, or flowers of the Dandelion are bruised, a milky-white juice, bitter to the taste, pushes out and soils the finger. Many plants have a milky juice in them, just as animals have red blood.

Dandelion flowers are formed in a more complicated way than the Rose and Tulip. You might first suppose the Dandelion flower to be double, many petals together forming a sun-whirl. But that is not the case. What one takes for a simple petal is in reality a complete, small, transformed flower. So a little Dandelion head is produced by many little flower parts. Since it looks as if many tiny flowers had been placed in a little basket, it is called a Basket flower. (Composite flowers are called in German "Basket flowers.") The plant family of the Composites (also called the Daisy family) is the largest of all and has an enormous number of varieties.

How can such a little flower basket be formed at all? Only by the sun's powerful help!

First, the earth tries to raise a little mound, as when it wishes to form a tree. But the process does not advance as far in the composites as in the case of a tree. Everything happens so quickly. Before a tree trunk can come forth from this little mound, the sun has already transformed it into a flower. Think of the flower base of a Composite, from which the many single flowers grow, as a little piece of the soil which the sun has separated off and transformed at once into a flower. It is really a little meadow. Since it is already plant-like and the sun has prepared it, flowers can grow out of it at once. There is no need first to form green leaves on this little meadow.

In this way a Dandelion head arises.

Imagine that all the little flower tubes have been cut and spread flat. In this way the yellow rays come into being. Each flower ray has five little teeth, since it is made up of five petals grown together. If you pull a single ray out of a Dandelion flower, you see that it extends underneath into a little tube, out of which pistil and stamens rise; the pistil is inferior and naturally very small, for only a single seed is contained within it.

From the tip of the pistil rise the long hairs which later form the feather crown of the parachute. The single flowers of a Dandelion head have no calyx, since all their calyxes have been put together, so that the whole little head may have an *involucrel* (forming a rosette surrounding the base of the flower cluster) calyx. This is green in color. When blooming time is past, the little Dandelion head folds up, the green calyx leaves lie close together, and above extends only a withered tuft which can be pulled off. Later it falls to the ground of its own accord. At this stage the heads generally incline toward the earth as if they were about to wither, but a new force—that of the ripening of the seed—lifts them up.

While the blossom is closed, the tips of the pistils lengthen out and push forward the flower crowns. At first the parachutes are folded up, but one day, when the calyx thrusts back again and the whole flower turns inside out, they spread apart. The "blow flower" is now formed.

Thus, from a bit of the earth which the sun had separated off, a little world has finally arisen. The flower base is the earth sphere. Over it arches a little starry sky made of many, tiny stars. There is much to be learned, too, from observing the green Dandelion leaves, which form a rosette on the ground below. You see from their many points and tips that they are formed by the light. An ordinary leaf would be simply egg-shaped, but the sun so pulls from all sides at the margin of the Dandelion leaf, that at length it looks as if it were fringed. From time to time a deeper indentation and a larger tooth appear.

So the sun works upon the Dandelion. It goes in waves over the leaf and draws out large and small points from the leaf margins. The Dandelion plant is soft and pulpy. It has no hard parts; right up to the blossom it is made wholly out of leaves. The sun is able to make the Dandelion so leafy, because in the spring it finds plenty of water in the earth. Then it needs only to give the plant its proper form and tousle the leaf margins to its heart's content.

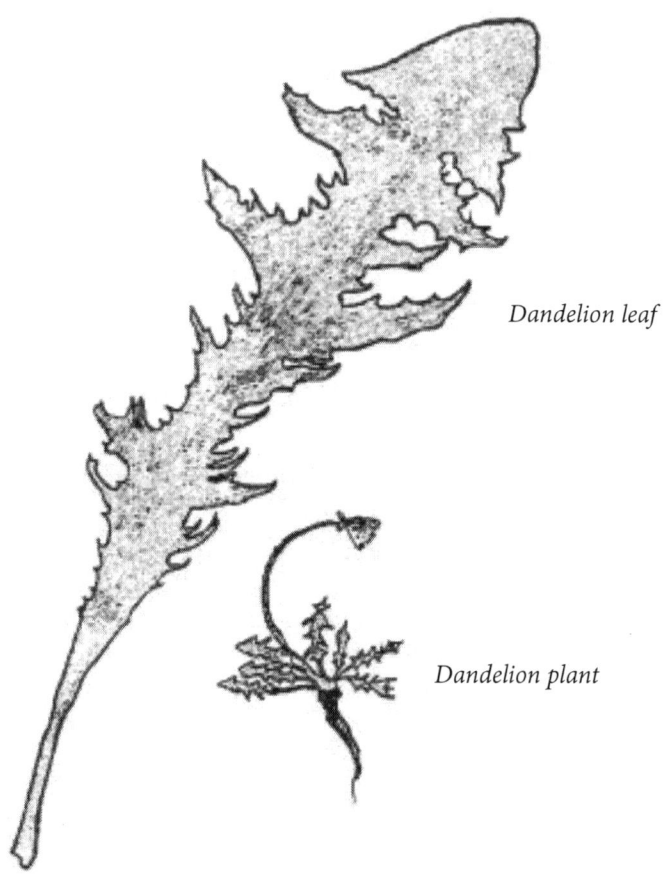

Dandelion leaf

Dandelion plant

Since the Dandelion, like the Tulip, flowers early in the spring, it also is in somewhat of a hurry about everything. So it quite forgets to form a stem. The flower stems of the Dandelion are not really stems but only their skin. Where the stem itself should be, the Dandelion has a hollow. It forgets to fill it in. Neither has it any stem leaves. And at the center of the leaves, where the midrib should be, there is also a hollow.

You may easily imagine what happens to the Dandelion when it forgets to form a stem. It just has to sit right down on the earth. And however beautifully formed are its leaves and shining its flowers, yet it cannot lift itself up. If the sun had not come and lifted the little flower baskets out of the earth, it would be a sorry sight. Looking at the great taproot, you would expect a high-reaching plant to spring forth from it. But you are surprised to find only a Dandelion.

The Dandelion blossoms are open only in the morning. They are finely sensitive to the sun. They might be called the tender hearts of the flowers, for they open with the rising sun and close their petals as with a gentle heartbeat.

They can do this only because they bear in themselves their white milky juice.

The Chicory

The Chicory (German: *Wegwarte*—wayfarer) has its name from the fact that it grows most happily along the roadside and on hard trodden grounds and rubbish heaps. You meet with it much less often in fields and meadow and never in the woods. Like the Nettle, it is one of those plants which follows the footprints of man. According to an old legend, it is an enchanted maiden who waits at the roadside in vain for her faithless loved one.

Not many plants arouse such a peculiar impression on closer acquaintance. First of all you see the blossoms, blue as heaven—the eyes of the longing maiden. They seem to hover in the air, for the plant to which they belong is not easily seen, especially since you expect a bunch of leaves and find only a hard skeleton of branches.

The Chicory flowers are like those of the Dandelion. They are also little "basket" flowers, only they are not yellow, but sky blue. Sometimes you find white or rose-colored Chicories, too. They open with the rays of the early morning sun, but even around noontime, in full sunlight, they close again. The Chicory has been called the "flower clock."

If you want to pick the flowers, you can't get them loose, for the Chicory stalks are exceedingly tough and solid. It seems inconceivable that these hard stalks belong together with the delicate flowers.

One must follow the whole development of the plant to understand it.

In the earth is fixed a powerful taproot, no less strong than that of the Dandelion. The green leaves are also very similar to those of the Dandelion. In the first year they form only a rosette, close to the ground. He who sees the plant striving upwards in the spring months of May and June is convinced of its strength. It pushes up a sappy leaf sprout. In the Chicory, as in the Dandelion plant, there is a white, milky juice. It tastes as bitter as gall.

If you know something of the bitter substances, you will understand the Chicory better. Bitterness draws everything together. So it is with the Chicory. When it has reached half of its height, it suddenly stops its growth and forms no more real leaves. It now takes on an altogether different appearance, and you can hardly imagine it as the same plant, for it becomes stalky and stretches long, thin shoots up into the air. These are the sturdy skeletons which later bear the blossoms. In spring, when the earth is still moist, the Chicory is also full of sap and has rich foliage. But when the earth gets dryer and warmer, the Chicory is transformed into a dry plant. Only now can the flower buds be placed upon it, for if they were to appear upon the rich shoots, they would bum up before they opened.

The Chicory blossoms have no stem, but sit directly on the branches. Several buds are drawn closely together because of the bitterness. When one blossom has faded, the next comes almost on the same spot. You have to look carefully to be sure it is not the same blossom. Each one blooms but half a day.

Were the Chicory not so bitter, each blossom could stretch out on a special little stem, and the Chicory would be a great, rich-branches bush. So, even externally, the Chicory shows you how bitter it is.

In many districts the Chicory is cultivated. The roots are harvested, broken up and roasted, to be used as a coffee substitute.

From the Chicory plant there is also prepared a medicine which works healingly when you have a sick stomach or if your intestines are not healthy. The juice of the acrid Chicory aids the digestion.

Finally, the sister of the Chicory, the Endive plant, must be mentioned. It is forced until it has young leaves. This gives the bitter Endive salad.

If the Chicory is compared to the Dandelion, to which it is related, the great contrast between the two plants is apparent. You could never imagine the Chicory blooming in May at the same time as the Dandelion. It does not begin to flower until July; then it continues up to the time of the frosts. The earth has first to become warm and dry. The Dandelion is a plant which has remained seated and has forgotten to form stalks. The Chicory develops a tall and spurting scaffold of branches, so that we can say that wherever the Dandelion has a gap, the Chicory has tough stems. It is a Dandelion filled in.

If you should want to transform a Dandelion into a Chicory, you would have to give it a stalk and change the color of the flowers from yellow to its complementary color, blue. But you would have to transfer it at the same time from spring to the warm summer, or the change would not take place.

Each plant is the child of its season.

The Autumn Crocus (*Colchicum autumnale*)

When summer is drawing to a close and the sun falls obliquely on the earth , since it describes a much smaller arc in the heavens, then the pale, lavender-colored Autumn Crocus blooms in the meadows. You can see from its fragile flower cup that it is the last bit of life that the sun can entice from the earth. The flowers are pale and weak and are easily bent over by the wind.

If you pick an Autumn Crocus, you also pull up from the earth the long flower tube into which the blossom merges. For, far below the ground, the Autumn Crocus has a bulb. If you try to dig it up, you will notice how deep down it lies. The colder the winter in a given region, the deeper the Autumn Crocus bulbs. They are like a thermometer of the average winter cold.

But what will strike you as most remarkable is that when the Autumn Crocus blooms, you find no green leaves on it. Only the faded flowers flicker like tiny, cold flames on the autumn meadows. If in the following May you go over the same meadows in which the Autumn Crocus grew, you will find large-leafed, sappy, green plants which look like tulips; and many people who do not know that these are the leaves of the Autumn Crocus wonder that so many Tulips grow in the meadows. They are confirmed in their error when they notice the sappy, green seed pods, which bear an extraordinary resemblance to a Tulip bud. But they are not flower buds, and you would wait in vain for them to open; they are the seed pods of the Autumn Crocus, which have developed from the flowers of the year before and have only just matured.

The whole development of the Autumn Crocus is delayed because it blooms at a time when the sun has very little power left. Between the flowering time and the ripening of the seeds comes winter; thus, the plant is torn asunder, as it were, into two equal halves.

If you compare the pale Autumn Crocus with the shining Spring Crocus, which it outwardly resembles, you will notice the difference. The Spring Crocus blooms when the sun-force is increasing; the Autumn Crocus blooms in the late fall, when the sun-force is rapidly decreasing. So the Spring Crocus is tight and strong, the Autumn Crocus pale and weary.

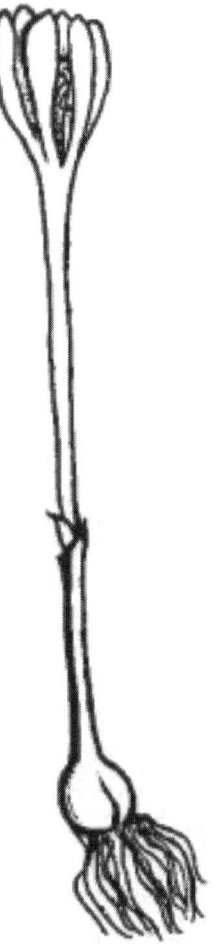

Autumn Crocus

Comparing the Autumn Crocus with the Tulip, you discover still another contrast, which corresponds with the contrasting blossom time. In the spring-blooming Tulip everything happens too fast, for the Tulip hurries to the flower stage, but in the case of the Autumn Crocus, everything goes much too slowly.

Not until autumn does it send its long, extended flower cup from the bulb into the air. It is six-parted, like that of the Tulip, and the stamens, also six in number, are fastened on the inner side of the flower crown.

There is something very curious about the stigma of the Autumn Crocus. There are three of them present. They are thread-like and run through the thin underground flower tube until within the bulb they are divided from each other. For while the flower crown and stamens are above in the light, the pistil of the Autumn Crocus is underneath in the bulb. Since the process goes so slowly, the pistil is stunted in its development and held fast when it tries to unfold. So it cannot emerge into the light with the other flower parts. You will also notice that the long, almost thread-like part, which connects the blossom above with the underground bulb, is not a flower stem but, rather, a greatly extended lower end of the flower crown with the pistil inside it.

Stalks and leaves of the Autumn Crocus are also, of course, quite undeveloped at the flowering time and are still deep down in the earth. Not until after their winter rest are they pushed up, taken hold of by the sun, and fully brought forth. The pistil is also pushed out and can now develop into a large, three-sectioned seed pod. At the top of the seed pod the dried remnants of the three stigma threads still stand, and you will also frequently see the remains of last year's blossom. Because the pistil of the Autumn Crocus is superior, the remains of the blossom hang from the lower end of the seed pod.

Is it any wonder that the Autumn Crocus is poisonous and spoils the fodder when there is too much of it! Like the Mushroom, it is penetrated too little by the sun when it blooms. It would very much like to be a Tulip, but it gets stuck half way.

The Countenance of the Earth

Plant life becomes changed where the sun no longer shines down upon the earth as it does here, and where moon and stars follow other courses. Summer and winter, day and night, pass differently, and tropical heat or polar cold gains the upper hand.

In our latitude the sun ascends the sky obliquely. It describes an arc which is larger in summer, in winter smaller, but never, even when it is highest, does it stand directly overhead in the zenith.

A very different picture is spread before the dwellers in lands lying nearer the equator. In the tropics the sun ascends vertically in the heavens and dips vertically again below the horizon in the evening. At the time of its greatest height it journeys in a line across the middle of the sky, and a post stuck in the ground at midday will throw no shadow at all, for the sun will be standing directly in line with it. At other seasons, too, it ascends much higher than it does in our latitude. How much more powerfully must its life-giving force work upon the earth in these tropical lands!

Where there is sufficient water—be it through the regular rainfall, by the borders of streams, or in swampy regions—it calls forth a plant growth whose luxuriance far exceeds anything known to us in our native regions, even those that are most fruitful.

Mighty trees form the main body of the primeval forests of the tropics. Giant crowns, teeming with a manifold world of animals, press one against another as their branches become entangled together. Only the strongest survive, and when such a giant tree breaks down or is uprooted, it tears with it whatever is nearby or underneath as it crashes to the ground. Each tree is like a garden, covered from top to bottom with other plants, with its bark scarcely visible anywhere. Climbing plants, like our Ivy or Wild Grape, creep up the trunks.

Twilight reigns among the trees, for the sunlight is almost spent before it can penetrate through the thick foliage. To this it must be added that in the dense, primeval, tropical forest it is very warm and moist, just as in a hothouse, where it sometimes seems you can hardly breathe if you are not used to the atmosphere.

Plants which love the shade form the undergrowth, but overhead in the tree tops a second plant world has grown up. Climbing growths, rooted in the earth, pull themselves up like ropes around the tree trunks, fling themselves from branch to branch and form wonderful garlands when they bloom. Others climb up to the highest tree tops, where, having reached bright daylight, they pour out a flower-rain of extravagant fullness and color.

Again, other tropical growths of the primeval forest take root right up in the tree crowns, where, in the axis of the branches, hollow trunks, etc., humus has been formed out of fallen leaves and rotted plant parts. Whereas in our country only moss and lichens thrive under such conditions, there flowering plants and great ferns grow side by side. You see, the sun can develop quite other and many more blossoms.

Only think of the Orchids! They often look like animals. Even their colors are flashy and uncanny. That is because of the moist heat.

This excessive growth force the earth, of course, has from the sun, which works much more strongly in these regions. Like a tidal wave the plant life wells up until a part of it is lifted to the tree tops, producing there a second luxuriant vegetation.

We get our most fiery aromatic plants from the tropics. Since the sun penetrates so far into the exuberant earth, all parts of the plant become intermingled. The flowering force reaches down into the leaves, roots, wood, and bark. The blossoms and fruits, too, have a special fire and a more delicious aroma.

It goes without saying that if the indispensable supply of water is lacking for the plant life of the hot countries, the vegetation picture completely changes—yes, even turns into its opposite. The up-welling forces subside, and the sun now works unmercifully, drying up the earth through its ardor—indeed, fairly turning it to a skeleton. In place of exuberance comes aridity; in place of the primeval forest, steppes or even deserts form.

A desert is a region in which almost no plants can grow; it is just the same whether the desert be of stone or sand. On the steppe at least grass thrives, always springing up fresh again during the brief rainy periods.

When the desert is mentioned, usually the Sahara comes first to mind, although extensive regions in lands other than Africa deserve this name. Not always is the desert necessarily unfruitful. It has often been shown, on the contrary, that man has been able by irrigation to transform the desert into land well suited for cultivation. Egypt will always remain the most instructive example of this kind. On the other hand, many fruitful regions have become desert land through the thoughtless intervention of man. Man has chopped down the woods in a self-seeking way. Then cloudbursts have come and washed away the soil, or the ground has perhaps dried out, having no longer a protecting roof of leaves; then it is an easy game for the wind to blow away the layers of soil. In this way many stone deserts have come into being.

The desert climate has transformed some plants in a most curious way, so that they can still live under such unfavorable conditions. They are greatly contracted, and either no longer have any leaves at all, or else their leaves are very small and fall off as soon as a brief rain is over. The rest of the time they stand as leafless bushes. The intense sunlight has invested them with many stout thorns, which make them impenetrable.

"Cushion" plants also grow in the desert. These rounded mats are anchored by very long taproots. Their trunks above ground are so thickly branched and so hardened that they remind you of little coral reefs rather than of plants. How would a widely branched plant with weak stalks and leaves, such as our Dead Nettle or Buttercup, be able to exist in a region of burning hot wind and deeply parched sand!

There is much to be learned from the Cactus plants, which—as is well-known—are native to the Mexican stone deserts. They no longer have any leaves, but only fleshy stem parts covered with a leathery skin. A Cactus has sucked its leaves into the swollen stem. That is why it is green. Some Cacti have taken on the leaf form and are pressed out flat.

The fragrant, mostly short-lived Cactus blossoms do not appear to belong at all to the solid stem parts bristling with thorns. Since a Cactus has no leaves, the blossoms have to sit right on the main stalk, and it looks as if something in between were missing—namely, the leaves. The Cactus behaves like its desert home, where the hot, light-filled air rebounds abruptly from the dead stone and there is no water to bring about a balance.

Now a Cactus has a great deal of fire-force stored up within it, though since it is a slow grower and very hard, you scarcely notice this. Not until the blossoms come out do you see how it fairly blazes.

Many tropical plants have developed to an extraordinary size. But still they have remained simple, as if the very heat had expanded their parts but had not carefully molded them. You can observe this in the Palms. Their large leaves, hard as the skin of a lizard, are less elaborated than some of our much smaller plants which grow in the meadows. Their trunks are not to be compared with those of our trees. They are rigid, unbranched columns. A Banana plant is nothing more than an herb grown to a giant size, with very simple leaves.

The steppes show in most striking form the contrast between moisture and dryness. With the onset of the rainfall they are wonderfully transformed in an amazingly short time. They are quickly covered with green, and everywhere gorgeous flowers spring forth from the ground, which before was a cheerless waste. You might imagine yourself suddenly transported to an enchanted land.

But the splendor does not last long. With the opening of the rainless summer, all the vegetation vanishes. Drought sets in. The bulbous plants withdraw under the earth, the grass dries out, and the seed-forming plants die down. A traveler has described the South African mountain desert during this season as the "most wretched, dried, burned up—as if charred in an oven—the most scorched, baked, consumed, god-forsaken region that the sun ever shone upon!" Others who have visited the same region in the rainy season have described it as a veritable wonderland. Could there be a greater contrast?

In the tropics each day is like a short summer. Since there is no winter there, but only a rainy season that varies from one region to the next, according to how the winds blow from the sea, you might also say that in the tropics the year has changed into the day.

The opposite is true of the polar regions. There the sun rises only once each year—in the spring. It then moves along low over the horizon without setting, reaching its highest position at the noontime of the polar day, which is also the middle of the summer. Then it slowly sinks down under the horizon again. A polar night lasts six months. Moon and stars, likewise, though in the tropics they rise vertically with the sun, are in the polar regions visible only in the winter and move in parallel circles above the horizon.

It is obvious to everyone that under such conditions the sun can penetrate only very weakly and for a short distance into the earth. And we know that great lands—inland parts of Greenland, for instance—stay covered with eternal ice, like layers of rock, since the warmth of the sun does not succeed in melting it, even though the summer is interrupted by no night.

When the first plant growth can stir, it remains nestled quite low on the earth's surface. A zone of Mosses and Lichens makes the start. The vegetation at first cannot yet go beyond this low stage of growth. In the tundra (the rolling, treeless plains of northern countries) formation, also, you find only small, dwarfed plants. There is no lack of water in these swampy regions, but neither the earth nor the sun can give them any robust life. In the tropics there are large and powerful growths, but they are often simple and unformed; the polar plants, on the contrary, though very small, are elaborated with the utmost care. They could be much larger and still look beautiful.

But what strikes you as very strange and gives to the polar regions the stamp of a desert landscape is the total absence of trees. No tree, no bush—far and wide. What a contrast to the tropical forest!

The earth is too weak to burgeon out. It can at best bring forth a superficial layer of plants. In many places it has only a thin, pale green covering.

The first trees are, as in lofty mountain regions, the Willows. They are the dwarf Willows, with tiny leaves and numberless little catkins. Their branches nestle like roots close to the ground, so that the bush presents much more the aspect of a cushion plant.

The first Spruce trees also have a very curious growth. Lacking the strength to stretch themselves upwards, they stay pressed against the ground and, spreading from a center, branch out over the earth. Only the tips of the branches rise up like little trees, and a single plant alone grows so that it looks like a whole thicket.

The non-wood fanning plants are contracted to dwarf size; then their parts become hardened and are elaborated to the utmost degree. They produce many varieties, for they are continually branching—both cushion and border plants, which often take on a spherical form.

Summer conjures forth from the low-lying cushion and border plants a full growth of flowers, whose colors are incomparably pure. The traveler who experiences this blossoming stands as before a miracle. The abundant blossoms collected here hover over the hardened plants like a second glorified stratum. Butterflies make their appearance and flutter over the flowery meadows trembling in the wind. It is as if they had literally been breathed into being. In contrast to primeval forest growths, Arctic plants are divided into two parts—an upper and a lower—wholly separated from the other. In the incomparably pure blossoms are reflected the star-bright polar heavens, but the hardened sprouts are the children of the almost petrified earth. It is as if a dividing line were drawn, as if heaven and earth could easily touch each other but could not interpenetrate. The contrasts between tropical and polar plants can easily be seen by placing their characteristics over against each other, as follows:

Tropics	Polar Regions
Warm pole	Cold pole
Living earth	Dead earth
Expanded plants	Contracted plants
Plant growth lifted into the air	Plant growth pressed down to the earth
Blossom-force submerged in the plants	Blossoms separated from the plants

In the temperate zones where we live, these contrasts interpenetrate one another. Day and night, summer and winter, regularly alternate. Here, it is true, grow neither the greatest number of plants nor the largest that are found on earth, but the life is most varied, and man has the widest choice of conditions in which to work.

Before this book is ended, a picture must be given of how much may be learned by ascending a high mountain, for each mountain comprises in itself a picture of the whole earth. The higher you go, the colder it grows, and the life of the earth becomes weaker. Over and against this weakening of the earth life, the heavens with their forces come nearer and nearer. Is it any wonder that the same flowers are found on high mountains as in polar regions? Especially if you have the good fortune to ascend a high mountain in the tropics, then you will see all the zones of the earth pass before your eyes, just as if you were making a complete but shortened journey from the north pole to the equator. After the eternal snow you come to a moss-lichen zone. Below it you reach the forests, similar to our mixed woodlands. Depending upon the location of the mountain, there may also be evergreen forests. Little by little the characteristic tropical vegetation begins to intermingle, until the lowlands are reached.

Our native mountains are also very instructive, only you must look at them in the right way. Are not our Gentians, Alpine Roses, and the many splendid varieties of Primroses formed exactly like the flowering plants of the polar regions? Cushion and border plants are be to found in great numbers. Many of these we plant in our rock gardens because of their loveliness and their profuse bloom. In them, as in the polar plants, their purely colored blossoms rest like a second layer upon the dwarfed, hardened sprouts. In trees and shrubs the woody parts are especially strongly developed and sprawl low over the ground.

Thus, the earth may be regarded as consisting of two giant-sized mountains, set with their bases against each other. Their summits are the two poles, and at the equator they come together.

Afterword for Adults

"The important thing is not that a thought can be found which is applicable everywhere, but that our understanding arrives at what is essential in an object or a living being."
—Rudolf Steiner

This book is intended for children and should be read by the children themselves. Nevertheless I believe that I owe some explanations to adults in regard to the striking—doubtless unusual—method of presentation.

I have written this book particularly for ten- and twelve-year-olds, yet experience will show that children of other ages—yes, adults themselves, I surely believe—will read the book with pleasure.

No single subject, whatever it may be, is without meaning for the development of the child's soul and spirit. It would perhaps be better to say that each subject has a very definite task to perform, which far exceeds its value as information.

There is but one pre-condition which must be fulfilled; the way in which a subject is handled—the method—must be a *living* one. It must be able to change with the child as he passes through different age levels. It is a very great delusion if someone supposes he has done justice to the nature of the child when he has simply prepared a thinned-out infusion of adult wisdom, only omitting what is "too advanced" for the child.

In a few words I shall endeavor to describe the principles which I hold to be the right ones. The content of the book itself will bear them out.

There are as many possibilities of leading up to the truths of the world as there are soul capacities. These capacities are fundamentally different in the child from what they are in the adult. Unfortunately, the modern adult is inclined to consider as "objective" only that abstract knowledge on which he has based his own intellectual activities. Herein lies an error which produces disaster for the child. He who wishes to carry on the study of plants with children must live in the realm of creative pictures as an artist does. The inner picture also speaks the truth, but otherwise than the intellect speaks it.

Attempting, as I have done, to set forth the life of the plant world in objective pictures, the one often evokes an understanding wink of the eye, implying assent that this method will perhaps do for children but would be unworthy—or even laughable—for adults, as it does not tally with the truth. As deadening as is the effect upon the child of giving him the pale picture of adult science, which he never really can take into himself, so is it also destructive to tell children a story which one rejects oneself as untrue. I should like expressly to remark that I am able to prove the truth in each of the pictures that I have used. Whenever the pictures are not mere playful imaginings, they develop within the child's soul as seeds which later, all by themselves, grow into something else. I should not withhold the fact that I owe most of the ideas of this book to my study of the works of the great pedagogue, Rudolf Steiner. A nine-year practice in teaching through all grade levels has taught me to revere the fruitfulness of these ideas, and I know how indebted I am to these spirit-born inspirations. Warmth of heart is the most natural trait of the child's soul. To suppose that one has first to produce this warmth through a childlike way of expression is to sin against the child's natural wholeheartedness. Unfortunately, the term "childlike" and "childish" are only too often confused. I have, therefore, refrained from speaking of the "dear Forget-me-not" and the "sweet little Violet," but have tried solely to let come to expression, through thought suggestions that will lead on further, the grace and charm inherent in the plants themselves.

Nothing further is necessary.

If sometimes questions occur to the adult reader: for instance, why some possible objections are not answered, why many things are only hinted at, why completeness is seemingly not striven for—let him first always examine himself whether such doubts do not perhaps arise from the intellectual, reflecting consciousness, not from the child himself, who sees things directly. In many instances I have given only hints to serve as food for thought and imagination.

In plant study it is necessary to make demands upon the child's capacity for thought and to develop it. Therefore, no reader should be puzzled by the prevalence of thought in the structure of this little book. Botany provides wonderful opportunities for referring to the larger interrelationships within the whole of life, and out of these considerations the details become clear of themselves. From the tenth year onward, the child begins to ask about the "why" of world phenomena, and plant study can lead him to answer such questions in a living way.

Unfortunately, it is impossible to express in a book much that will unfold very naturally in the course of personal contacts with children. The pictures required for such descriptions would appear distorted and be exposed to misunderstanding. But it is just these intimate things which most of all link the child's interest with the life of plants. Let the reader bear in mind that we have here deliberately restrained ourselves.

Moreover, there is a difference between the spoken and the written word. A child is, above all, convinced when he has before him the impression of a personality, hears the tones of the voice, perceives facial expressions and gestures. The printed text, also, has to be much more concise and unequivocal than the spoken word in a classroom lesson. The paragraphs must be read repeatedly, and each time a picture must arise before the mind of the child.

Much more might be said about plants and children, and really ought to be said. But since this little book has a different objective, I must let the matter rest with these few indications. If the adult wishes to learn what form practical plant study, as indicated here, assumes when set forth in botanical concepts for the more developed understanding, my other writings may be recommended to him: above all, the two small volumes, *Metamorphoses in the Plant Realm* and *Metamorphoses of Flowers*. There he will find a great deal set forth which could not be included in the present little book.

Made in the USA
Middletown, DE
23 September 2025